Fish and
How They Reproduce

Fish and
How They Reproduce

by Dorothy Hinshaw Patent

drawings by Matthew Kalmenoff

HOLIDAY HOUSE · *New York*

Library of Congress Cataloging in Publication Data

Patent, Dorothy Hinshaw.
  Fish and how they reproduce.

  Bibliography: p. 123
  Includes index.
  SUMMARY: Describes the general characteristics of
different kinds of fish with emphasis on their varied
reproductive processes.
    1. Fishes—Reproduction—Juvenile literature.
[1. Fishes. 2. Reproduction] I. Kalmenoff, Matthew.
II. Title.
QL639.2.P38   597'.01'6   76-10349
ISBN 0-8234-0285-1

To Joe and Mabel Patent,
the best in-laws ever

Contents

1 · The Variety of Fish

The word "fish" makes us think of many things—a scary shark cruising near a beach, a tank full of colorful tropical pets, a tasty fried trout for dinner, and more. The variety of fish life is equally diverse, as are man's links with the world of fish. They are our friends, our enemies, and also our ancestors. Although we feel little closeness to their unblinking, scaly coldness, we are curious about them.

One of the most interesting aspects of fish life is how young fish are brought into the world. The great success of fish in populating the waters of the world is due in large part to the variety of ways they reproduce. There seem to be all the variations that are possible.

In a great number of species, the male and female go through elaborate courtship rituals before mating, while in a few kinds the male has been altogether eliminated. Many fish, such as the stickback, lay only a few eggs which are guarded carefully against enemies, while still others, like the guppy, retain the eggs in their bodies and give birth to baby fish. Species such as herring simply lay tens of thou-

*Sluggish armored animals, the ostracoderms, were the remote an-
cestors of modern fish. The appearance of these three examples was
deduced from their fossils.*

sands of eggs each year. Chance takes over from there. The young of many fish resemble their parents closely, but others must pass through a totally different larval stage before transforming into adults. We will explore fish reproduction in all its fascinating variety, but first we must get to know our subjects as living things.

The First Vertebrates

We think of living fish as a single group of aquatic animals with fins and gills, but in reality they are as diverse in origin and form as four-legged land animals. In order to understand these differences, let us take a quick look at the evolution of fishes—where they come from and how they have changed through the ages.

The first fishlike creatures are found as fossils about 500 millions years old. Scientists have been unable to agree on what kind of animal was the direct ancestor of these small, jawless animals. They were ostracoderms—shell-skinned animals—and probably led a dull, quiet life, lying on the bottom of fresh-water swamps, sucking mud to get food. They probably moved very little, for their bodies were covered with hard, bony armor, and their fins were not well developed. There were a few heavy scales near the tail. Being small and slow and having no jaws to defend themselves, these early fish needed their armor as protection against large and hungry invertebrate predators of the time.

Modern Descendants

Some descendants of the ancient, heavily armored, sluggish ostracoderms are scaleless and boneless—the hagfish and lamprey. They are called cyclostomes, or "roundmouths." Over the millions of years since ostracoderms were plentiful, the heavy scales were eliminated and cartilage—a somewhat soft but tough kind of tissue—replaced the skeleton's bone. These primitive fish do, however, show many signs of their ancient ancestry. They have no jaws or true teeth. They have one nostril instead of two, and they lack paired fins. Rows of openings along their bodies connect to gill pouches for breathing.

Although they are both eel-like in appearance and have slimy skins, hagfish and lampreys are quite different. The two diverged long ago in their evolution. Hagfish are sea-dwelling scavengers. They have a well developed sense of smell which leads them to the dead and dying fish that they eat more than any other kind of food. Fleshy projections on their snouts probably also aid in locating food—which is fortunate for them, for their eyes are pratically useless. The biggest hagfish are about thirty inches (75 centimeters) long. If they are disturbed, they produce a great deal of slippery slime, which makes them poor targets for predators. Hagfish lay large, yolky eggs which hatch into young similar in appearance to the adults.

Lampreys, on the other hand, all spawn small eggs in fresh water and have a strange larval form. Some live in the sea as adults, but others spend their whole lives in fresh water. Many kinds of lampreys are parasites. They use their wide, sucker-like mouths to latch onto other fish Once attached, the lamprey cuts away with its hard, sharp, horny "teeth" until it is firmly imbedded in the tissues of its victim. Glands at the back of the mouth send out chemicals which prevent the host's blood from clotting, and the lamprey literally sucks its victim dry.

The sea lamprey, which also thrives in fresh water, has been a serious economic pest in the United States. Before 1829, Niagara Falls kept these parasites out of the Great Lakes. But in that year, Canada completed the Welland Canal, which allowed ships to enter the lakes from the ocean. Unfortunately, the lampreys entered as well. By the 1950s the commercial fish catch in the Great Lakes was down to almost nothing, due to a combination of pollution and lampreys. In previous years, as much as 18 million pounds (a pound is about half a kilogram) had been harvested. Much of the decline was due to the very efficient sea lamprey parasite, which made the results of years of pollution even worse. In recent years a battle has been waged against the lampreys and the pollution-producers. As of today the Great Lakes are steadily improving as fishing grounds.

Modern Fish Evolve

About 400 million years ago, while ostracoderms were still plentiful, another group of armored fishes, called placoderms, appeared. They had one important trait which ostracoderms lacked—jaws. With jaws, they could become more active animals, capable of snapping up food and defending themselves. The variety of placoderm types was tremendous. Most have died off without leaving ancestors. But scientists believe that some type of placoderm gave rise to ancestors of the jawed fish we have today in our oceans, lakes, and fishbowls.

Although scientists have yet to discover a complete series of fossils showing how vertebrates evolved, two very important characteristics of vertebrates appeared about this time, jaws and two pairs of fins. With the evolution of these features, the basic arrangement of all vertebrates other than cyclostomes was laid down. The spinal column running along the top side of the animal, protecting the nerve cord and supporting the body, is connected by various bones to the bones of the four limbs. At the head end of the body is an expanded region of nervous tissue, the brain, which regulates the activities of the animal and which is protected by an encasing skull. The movable jaw of vertebrates enables them to capture, hold onto, and chew their food very efficiently. From sharks on up the evolutionary scale, vertebrates show many different forms, but all types are variations on this very basic architecture.

Very early in the evolution of fish with jaws, two separate lines of development arose. The cartilage fish—sharks and their relatives—form one branch. Through the ages, the bony outer armor of the placoderm ancestor was reduced to a covering of small toothlike scales. The bony

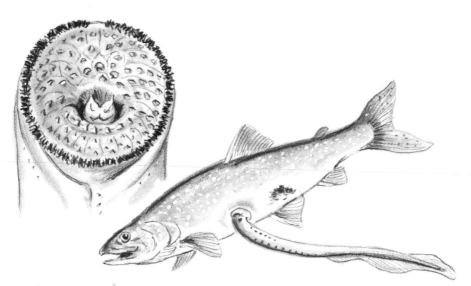

The lamprey, top, attaches itself to a fish with its sucker mouth and sucks its victim dry. The mouth with its toothlike rasp is shown in close-up. The head of the hagfish, below, has smelling organs that lead it to dead or dying fish.

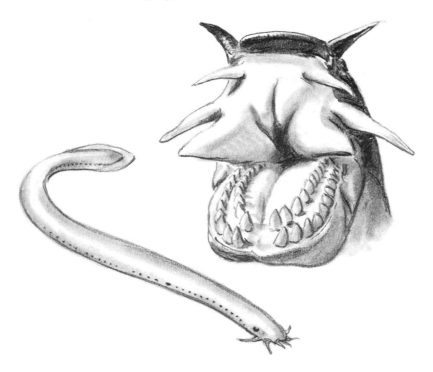

skeleton was lightened and reduced to a skeleton of cartilage. We think of sharks as being primitive fish, but their
light, flexible skeleton is not a primitive feature. In appearance and way of life, however, modern sharks are very
similar to those which roamed the seas 150 million years
ago.

Early in evolution, sharks developed an efficient body
layout which enabled them to be successful predators of the
sea. Most modern sharks are still deadly killers, but a few
have become adapted to a more peaceful life, filtering
small animals out of the sea with special gill rakers. The
sharp, light scales of sharks provide protection against
attack without adding much weight. Their many rows of
strong, curved teeth are not fused to their jaw cartilage, and
are replaced as they wear out. And sharks' eyes are able to
distinguish moving shapes well in the dim waters below
the surface where they live.

Skates and rays are shark relatives which have adopted
a different way of life. Their bodies and fins are very flattened, and their tails are long and thin. Some species are
dangerous to humans. The electric rays produce a strong
electric current in specially modified muscle tissue which
can give a bad shock. Stingrays have poisonous spines in
their tails which can kill a human. But most skates and
rays are totally harmless to us. The majority spend their
lives quietly on the sea floor, feeding on fish and shellfish.
A few species, such as the magnificent manta ray, swim
almost continuously, straining minute food organisms from
the water.

The chimeras, or ratfish, are a strange group of cartilage fish. Although they are usually considered to be evolved from sharklike ancestors, some scientists feel they developed from a separate placoderm ancestor. They have strong jaws and teeth which they use to crush the shells of clams and sea urchins. Their skin feels soft and slippery instead of sharp and hard. Although ratfish-like fossils 200 million years old have been found, little is known about the chimeras' way of life today.

Bony Fish

The other main branch of fish evolution is the bony fish. This group is by far the most successful of all fish types. Ninety-five per cent of living fish belong to this group, and one branch of bony fishes gave rise to amphibians and therefore to all higher vertebrates.

The first bony fish appeared much earlier than did the first sharks. While cartilage fish were found mainly in the oceans, bony fish probably evolved at first in fresh water. Later on they successfully invaded the sea. Primitive bony fish had lungs which helped them to get oxygen while living in stagnant water and to survive periods of drought. In most modern bony fish, the lung has been converted into the gas-filled swim bladder.

Near the beginning of bony-fish evolution, two branches diverged. The lobe-finned fish are mainly of historical importance, for they led to the amphibians. Present-day lungfishes and the "living fossil" coelacanth are the only surviving lobe-finned fish. The other branch of bony fish consists of those that are ray-finned. There are several minor groups of these, such as the gars, sturgeons, and paddlefish. But the vast majority of living fish belong to the highly varied and successful group called teleosts.

Teleost Success

Ninety per cent of the present-day fish are teleosts. Some 20,000 teleost species are known. The little anchovy and the huge marlin and tuna are teleosts. Ordinary-looking fish like trout and bass are teleosts, as are strange ones such as sea horses, puffer fish, and eels. Cartilage fish are swimming predators, plankton feeders, or bottom-dwelling types. Few live in fresh water. Bony fish other than teleosts are few in number and live limited lives. But teleosts can be found in almost all watery habitats, fresh and salt. They live in arctic waters of 30° F. (-1° C; sea water freezes at a lower temperature than fresh water) and hot springs over 100° F. (over 38° C).* They inhabit shallow tide pools and deep ocean trenches. Some teleosts survive in very stagnant water, and others live in pools that dry up every year. Teleosts are predators, vegetarians, scavengers, and parasites. What has enabled them to adapt to so many ways of life?

Scientists have marveled over this question for a long time. It is the kind of question which cannot be answered

* The centigrade (Celsius) scale is used internationally in ordinary use; the related Kelvin scale, which is used scientifically for the very highest accuracy, is the basic scale in the metric system.

with any certainty, for it concerns events of the past. No experiments can be performed to tell which ideas are correct, but we can learn something from considering the possibilities.

One factor which probably contributed to teleost success is size. While the smallest sharks are six inches (15 centimeters) long, and most kinds are at least five or six feet in length (six feet equal about two meters), most teleosts are from one inch to one foot long (two and a half centimeters to about one-third meter). A small fish can live in many places such as shallow water or rocky reefs where a large fish cannot. Small fish also reach maturity faster and can breed more rapidly and in larger numbers.

Another advantage of the teleost is the swim bladder, which evolved from the lung of teleost ancestors. The swim bladder varies from one group of teleosts to another, but basically it is a gas-filled sac which acts like ballast, enabling the fish to adjust its density to that of the surrounding water. A teleost with an efficient swim bladder is in effect weightless and does not need to expend any energy in maintaining its position in the water. Its fins (see glossary for fin descriptions) are thus freed from constant movement and can be used for fast, delicate maneuvering instead.

The teleost brain has also developed to serve a fast-paced life. It is more highly developed than the brain of a shark. There are more cross-connections between the sensory and motor parts of the brain. This allows the quick escape responses necessary to a small fish. It also increases the flexibility of the fish's behavior, which has helped teleosts adapt to so many environments.

2 · The World of the Fish

Next time you go for a swim, try to imagine what it would be like to be a fish. Your body feels light; you do not "fall" to the bottom. The denseness of water gives support. If you open your eyes under water, things look blurry because your eyes are adapted for seeing in air. If you walk along the bottom, you must struggle against the weight of the water.

These and other properties of water have shaped and limited the form and life style of fishes. Because of the incompressibility of water, fish which spend much time swimming are very streamlined. Their noses are pointed, and their bodies are smoothly curved. They are widest in the middle and gradually taper off to a thin tail. This tapering allows the water to slip smoothly past the fish with little turbulence.

The skin of fish is very different from ours. The outer layer of our skin consists of dead cells which protect the inner living layer from drying out. Since fish live in water, they do not need this protective outer layer. Fish skin is alive. The scales, remnants of the heavy bony armor of the first fishes, are actually under the outer layer of the skin, not over it. Most fish feel slippery. This is because they are covered with mucus, a slimy substance produced by special cells of the skin. The mucus helps the animal slip easily through the water, and it usually protects the skin from infection by fungi and parasites.

Because the density of water is almost the same as that of protoplasm, fish are in effect practically weightless. Therefore they can have a light, flexible skeleton. Hagfish, lampreys, sharks, skates, rays, and ratfish all have a cartilage skeleton. But the great flexibility of cartilage limits the possible forms its possessors can take on. The bony fish, especially teleosts, are far more variable in shape, partly because bone can provide a sturdy framework for more modifications of shape than cartilage can.

Breathing in water is a fairly simple proposition for fish. Water is taken into the mouth and passed over gills, where very fine blood vessels run close to the surface. The hemoglobin in the blood picks up oxygen from the water, and waste materials pass out from the blood into the water at the same time. Teleosts take the water into their mouths and push it backward over the folds of gill filaments, which are covered by the operculum, or gill cover. Water goes out through the slits behind the opercula.

The gills of sharks are not covered by opercula. Instead there are several gill slits along the sides of the head through which water makes its exit. Because they use their mouths in breathing, teleosts cannot chew their food in them, or

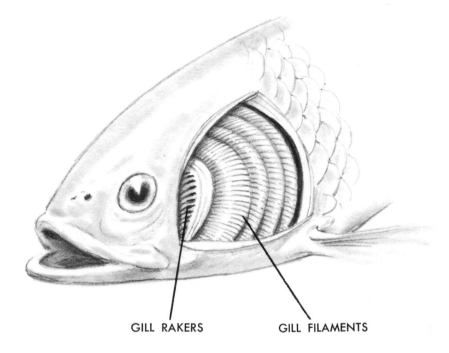

GILL RAKERS   GILL FILAMENTS

Beneath the gill cover—removed in this view—can be seen the gill rakers, which keep food particles from being lost and protect the gills from hard particles; next to them are the gills, usually four on each side of the animal. The gills receive oxygen from the water and release waste chemicals into it before it passes out from under the gill cover.

they would suffocate. Their mouth teeth can hold or crush food, but teleosts which also need to chew have special grinding teeth in their throats, behind the gills, where they cannot interfere with respiration. Sharks simply tear off chunks of food with their powerful jaws and swallow them whole.

Senses of Fish

Vision is simpler for fish than for land-living animals. When light rays enter a liquid from the air, they are bent. Since the inside of the eye is liquid, land vertebrates have a cornea and a lens which can change shape to help adjust for the bending of the light rays. Fish, however, have a spherical lens and no cornea. Since they live in water, the light rays come straight into their eyes without bending. The lens can be moved backward for whatever focusing is necessary. Fish eyes also lack the tear ducts and eyelids of land dwellers. The water in which they live keeps their eyes moist and clean.

The eyes of most fish protrude a bit from the sides of the head, giving them all-around vision. They can see up, down, in front, or in back with ease. Food or enemies approaching from any direction are seen immediately. Unlike land animals, fish do not need necks to enable them to see everywhere.

Most fish have quite a good sense of smell. It is useful in finding food and detecting enemies. In some species, chemicals can carry a message from one individual to another. For example, if a minnow is injured, a chemical from its skin is released which panics the other minnows in the school. This "alarm substance" warns the fish quickly of danger. Taste is also highly developed in many fish. In addition to taste buds in their mouths, the barbels—slender, fleshy feelers—of fish such as catfish and sturgeons are studded with taste buds, so they can savor food before it even enters their mouths. American catfishes, mullet, and cod even have taste buds on their body skin. If one touches the side of a cod with a piece of meat it will turn and snap it right up.

Most fish have another sensory system which does not exist in land animals. It is called the lateral-line system. One can see the lateral line along each side of a fish, running from the gill opening to the tail. It also has several branches around the head, but these are usually buried in the skull bones and cannot be seen. For many years, scientists debated the function of this mysterious system. It was hard for them to imagine what it might do, since land animals lack it. Although it is not completely understood even now, the lateral-line system is known to detect low-frequency vibrations and pressure waves. Such waves occur when a solid object moves through the water. Through this set of organs the animal can detect the presense of other fish. Also, the waves produced by the fish itself as it swims bounce off solid objects like an echo. In this way it can "hear" the location of rocks and other objects in the water.

There was a time when people thought fish could not hear at all. No ears are visible on a fish's head, so how could it hear? Fish lack the highly developed and delicate middle ear which enables mammals to hear so well. But fish can hear, some of them better than others. Cartilage fishes and most bony fishes can perceive a limited range of sound through the inner ear. Water is a better conductor of sound waves than air, so hearing is possible for fish even with their underdeveloped ears. But about 5000 species of teleosts have a much improved sense of hearing. The swim bladder of carp, catfish, and some others is hooked up to the ear by a series of tiny movable bones. In others, such as tarpon and squirrel-fish, small branches of the swim bladder reach forward and contact a thin-walled part of the ear capsule. Sounds in the water cause the swim bladder to vibrate, and these vibrations are passed on to the ear. The swim bladder thus functions in a way similar to our eardrum.

The Intelligence of Fish

We think of fish as simple vertebrates. Although their brains are much less developed than those of mammals, teleost fish manage to live quite complicated lives. Cyclostomes and cartilage fish have considerably simpler brains than teleosts, and because of their size and habitat, scientists have had little chance to study their ways. The behavior of teleosts, which are important as food and valued as aquarium pets, has been investigated in some detail.

The behavior of an animal has two parts—the learned part and the "instinctive" part. "Instinct" is a vague word which has been used in so many ways that scientists tend to avoid it. They prefer to use the word "innate" instead of "instinctive." Innate behavior is not learned; it is built into the nervous system of the animal. Learned behavior is behavior which has been modified by experience. Although a few scientists still argue over the relative importance of learned and innate behavior in the lives of animals, most now agree that there is a close interaction of learning with the inborn responses of an animal which results in its final behavior.

For example, if a male guppy is raised by himself with

no other fish in his tank, he still will perform the normal courtship behavior when he is grown up and placed in a tank with other guppies. He did not have to learn the behavior pattern from watching other males courting females. However, at first he will direct his courtship to male fish as well as to females. He did not have a chance to learn where to direct his display. The behavior pattern itself in this case is basically innate, but its proper use must be learned.

Teleosts show a great variety of behavior which is probably largely innate. They have complex mating rituals involving many different kinds of signals which are mutually understood by the fish involved. Many fish form schools and others undergo long migrations. But learning is important in the lives of fish, too. Salmon learn the scent of their home stream and remember it for years. Male fish learn the boundaries of their territories and stay within them. Fish can learn when and where food is abundant. They can learn to avoid enemies as well. This combination of quite fixed behavior patterns and learning which lends flexibility to their lives has been an important part of the teleost secret of success.

Three fish of the ocean depths: from top to bottom, a saber-toothed viper fish, a candelabra sea devil, and Photostomias guernei *(it lacks a common name). In this habitat, such adaptations as lighted lures that attract prey are important, as are efficient teeth for capturing and holding the relatively few prey animals that are available.*

The Variety of Aquatic Habitats

The adaptability of the teleosts can best be seen when we consider the variety of their habitats. We are all aware of how varied land environments are, from barren, snow-capped mountains to sultry, teeming rain forests; from frozen northern tundra to dry, burning deserts. Aquatic habitats are at least as varied. Besides the obvious differences between salt and fresh water and between arctic seas and tropical lagoons, there are other equally radical contrasts.

One is the great increase in pressure and decrease in light intensity as water gets deeper. The fish which live in the ocean depths lack a swim bladder, for example. Because of the extreme pressure, their bodies are equal in density to water without the bladder. Often deep-sea fish have large eyes and special light organs that provide a built-in flashlight. Food is scarce deep in the sea, and these fish often have huge mouths that let them take advantage of a meal of any size when it comes along. Altogether, their world is a monotonous one, with little change in the temperature, pressure, and darkness of the water.

Fish which live in shallow seas have a totally different kind of life. Their habitats include many different living things and a varied "landscape" of reefs, cliffs, ridges, mountains, and plains. Water temperature and light intensity vary with the time of day and season. Food is more abundant, but so are dangers.

Fresh-water life has great variety as well. A stream-dwelling trout has a different life from the lake-living perch. The annual fish of hot, muddy ponds live a totally strange existence, quite different from that of the inhabitants of cold, permanent mountain lakes. Many adaptations are necessary for all this, and the reproductive habits of these different sorts of fish are among the most important ones that help suit them to survival in their environments.

3 · Making More Fish

The most crucial time in the life of any living thing is the period when it reproduces. Only when it passes its traits on to offspring is a plant or animal truly successful. A strong, healthy individual which fails to reproduce dies leaving no trace of itself on the earth.

Realizing this, we can see that every living thing reproduces in a way suited to its own particular life style. Since fish have evolved so many different ways of life, we should not be surprised to see how varied their reproductive habits are.

Casual Mating

Many deep-sea fish and fish which live in the open ocean lay large numbers of eggs which float to the surface. There they join the rich surface collection of living things —usually quite small—called the plankton. Mating behavior is simple but the number of eggs it produces is considerable. The Atlantic mackerel, for example, lays about

The Atlantic mackerel lays an enormous number of eggs each year.

a half million eggs a year. Since she lives for four years, the female lays about two million eggs in her lifetime. Only two of these must survive to adulthood to replace her and a male fish. The mortality of young mackerel is tremendous— only about one in a million survives to reproduce. The causes of death are many. Some eggs do not get fertilized in the brief and casual pairing of the fish. Others are destroyed by fungal and bacterial diseases, while many are eaten by other organisms living in the plankton, such as jellyfish and arrowworms. Other eggs may drift into water that is too warm or too cold for their normal development to occur. These same fates overtake large numbers of the young fish as well. Those which survive the dangers of planktonic life risk becoming some other creature's dinner at some time throughout their lives.

Other ocean fish, such as the winter flounder, lay eggs which sink. These eggs are larger in size and fewer in number than floating eggs. They can contain more heavy yolk to nourish the embryos since they do not have to float. These fish lay hundreds or thousands of eggs instead of the hundreds of thousands, or even millions, laid by most species with planktonic eggs and larvae. The young fish which hatch from sinking eggs tend to stay on the bottom in shallow waters where there is lots of food.

Protective Parents

Many fish which live in shallow waters lay fewer eggs, which they protect from danger to varying degrees. Often such eggs are attached to rocks or plants. This makes them resist being dragged away by tides, but they are easier for predators to find. The guarding parent can prevent them from being eaten.

Salmon migrate to the shallow upper reaches of rivers and streams where few predators live, and bury their eggs in the sand for further protection. Many reef fish and lake fish lay eggs which they guard until hatching, and a surprising variety of fish protect their young for days or weeks after they have emerged into the world.

Very different and sometimes striking methods are used to protect eggs. In a few fish, such as the popular aquarium angelfish, both parents guard the eggs and young. More often one parent does the job. Males of some minnows, sun-

fish, cichlids, gobies, sticklebacks, reef fish, and others protect their nests from predators. The mouth is used by
many fish species as a safe nursery for the eggs and sometimes the young fish as well; some sea catfish, cave fish,
cichlids, and cardinal fish use this convenient technique.

Certain fish protect their eggs by carrying them about
on their bodies. The female sea horse lays her eggs in a
special pouch on the male's belly, and he carries them along
until they hatch. Various sea horse relatives, such as pipe-
fish, also have pouches. Sometimes the female instead of
the male has the pouch. The peculiar humphead male has
a hooklike, nearly circular ring sticking out from the front
of his head. When this river fish from New Guinea mates,
the twisted cord of eggs is looped through the eye of the
hook, and the male carries the egg clusters around until
they hatch. The female of some catfish lies down on the eggs
after spawning. They sink into her soft, spongy skin and
are carried until hatching.

Other fish hide their eggs in the bodies of totally unrelated animals. The European bitterling deposits eggs inside the shell of a fresh-water mussel. The male fish selects
a mussel to his liking and guards it. The female has a long
egg-laying tube which she sticks down between the two
halves of the mussel, depositing the eggs in the gill chamber. The male releases his sperms in the water, where they
are sucked into the gills by the mussel. Marine fish are
known which lay eggs inside the gill chamber of crabs.
There they receive a fresh current of water and are completely protected from enemies.

One fish, the spraying characid, has been observed in

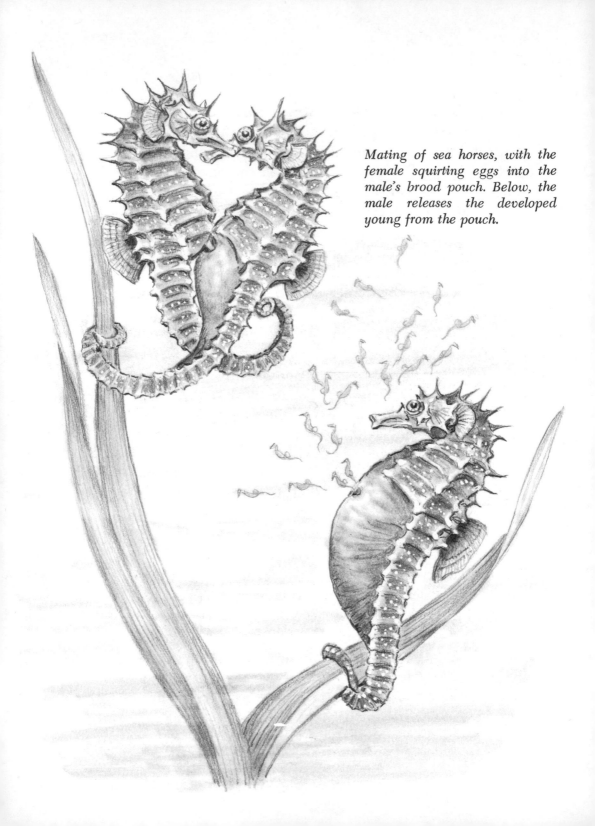

Mating of sea horses, with the female squirting eggs into the male's brood pouch. Below, the male releases the developed young from the pouch.

aquariums in something highly unusual: it actually lays its eggs out of the water. The mating pair jump together and cling to a leaf overhanging the water. They stick for a few seconds, apparently using their fins in some way to hang on while the eggs are laid and fertilized. This act is repeated many times. Each batch of eggs is carefully laid near the others until about sixty to a hundred eggs cover an area of about the size of a silver dollar. The female swims away, while the male begins his parental duties. He stations himself near the bottom of the aquarium on the opposite side

The long ovipositor, or egg-laying tube, of the European bitterling puts her eggs into a ready-made "safe-deposit vault."

from the eggs. But every twenty minutes or so he dashes over to them and splashes water up onto them with his strong tail, preventing them from drying out. Then he returns to his waiting place. When the young hatch in two or three days, they fall into the water. His job completed, the male fish then swims away.

Several unrelated groups of fish have evolved ways of bearing live young—a method called viviparity. They generally have fewer offspring than guarding fish, for the eggs are never exposed to the dangers of water life. Live-bearing fish are found in many different habitats. Many sharks are live-bearers, along with some small shallow-water marine fishes and fresh-water species. Live-bearing species are also found in the deep sea. Some of the viviparous species, such as guppies and platties, have become popular aquarium fish because they are so easy to breed.

Courtship and Mating

In order for an egg to divide and form an embryo, it must unite with a sperm cell (there are a few exceptions to this rule, however). In the great majority of fish, the males and females are separate individuals which must be brought together at mating time. The male either places the sperm inside the body of the female where it can fertilize the eggs, or he releases his sperm into the water at the same time the female lays the eggs, or right after she lays them. Fish have various types of courtship and mating behavior which assures that a ripe female and a ripe male will release their eggs and sperm together and insure a high rate of fertilization of the eggs.

Besides synchronizing the release of eggs and sperm, courtship behavior assures that the fish which mate are of the same species. The male of each fish species has his own signals which are understood by the female. And the female has signals which the male recognizes. In nature, it is very rare for two species to cross-breed. When they do, the embryos usually do not develop properly. Even if they do grow into adults, the adults often are sterile and cannot themselves reproduce. So if a fish makes a mistake and mates with a fish of a different species, its eggs or sperm are wasted. Because of this danger, species which live together in the same area have distinctly different courtship behavior. This insures that they will mate with their own kind.

Usually the male is more active in courtship than the female. He must convince her to mate with him, for she has to cooperate if mating is to be successful. Male fish such as the guppy are brightly colored and dance around the female displaying their finery to get her attention. Since guppies breed the year round, the male is always brightly colored.

During the breeding season, male fish of other kinds often develop bright colors. Their ordinary drab, protective colors are transformed into brilliant reds, greens, or blues. This "breeding dress" tells other males that here is a fish ready to defend his territory. It tells the female fish that this male is ready to mate. And it enables the breeding males to recognize the duller female fish easily.

Mating fish use other cues besides color. The swollen abdomen of the female, full of eggs, may also attract the male. Males and females often have differently shaped fins. And the behavior of a fish is also an indication of its sex. A female fish ready to mate behaves differently from a male or an unripe female.

Many teleosts can change color in a flash. These color changes can carry messages, too. Usually an aggressive fish will have brighter though darker colors, and a submissive, frightened fish will have pale colors. The position of the fins can also signal a fish's mood. While an aggressive fish will spread out its fins, a submissive one will fold them. These and other signals enable fish in the breeding season to communicate clearly with one another.

The details of courtship and territorial behavior are different for each teleost species. However, the displays of many species follow a few general rules. In many, the male fish stakes out a certain area of his own at breeding time. This is his territory, which he defends against other males of his kind. If another male comes near, the resident rushes over and threatens him.

Threat displays vary, but the lateral display is common. The resident fish approaches the intruder and spreads his fins out as far as he can, making himself look as big as possible. He swims slowly and deliberately around his opponent. If the other fish does not retreat, the resident may beat him with his tail. Some fish also have a frontal display. The male rushes at his enemy with his gill covers spread and his mouth wide open. Such species often have prominent eyelike color spots on the gill covers which add to the impression of large size. Usually the other male leaves without a fight. If he does not, the two fish may have a mouth to mouth wrestling contest or a fin-slapping bout until the weaker fish leaves. The resident male almost always wins these contests.

A breeding territory is handy for several reasons. Once territories are set up, there is little fighting among the males, so mating can proceed without disturbance. Females can easily find mates by visiting the area of the territories. And often the territory also provides a safe, protected place for laying eggs and raising young.

Some fish appear to use light instead of color as a means of communication. Many kinds of fishes living in the sea have light-producing organs. The light organs of a male lantern fish are on the upper part of his tail, while the female carries hers below. The different flashes of the two sexes are easy to tell apart. The flashlight fish carries a headlight under each eye. It has a lid which can cover the light, so it can control the flashing easily. The female flashlight fish appears to use her light to drive intruders away, and further studies may show that it is used in courtship as well.

Although vision is the most important sense in fish courtship, some species have other kinds of signals. The male toadfish makes a grunting sound which apparently declares his territory to other males. He has a more pleasant call which sounds like a boat whistle and which attracts the female. Sound is thought to be important in the communication of other fish, such as some cichlids, as well.

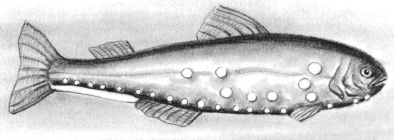

Many deep-sea fish have common names involving words like "flash-light" and "lantern." At top is Photoblepharon palpebratus, *a flash-light fish; the white patch (photophore) beneath each eye gives off light from a colony of bacteria living in the organ. There are more than 170 species of the lantern fish* Myctophum, *below, each with its own pattern of photophore arrangement. This is a female, with a large photophore beneath its tail.*

In the case of the blind cave-fish of Mexico, the female produces a chemical which excites the male. Other fish probably have similar chemicals. Scientists have begun to study communication in electric fish. These animals produce an electric field around their bodies and can sense objects nearby by the changes in that field. They also react to the electric signals produced by other fish, and will answer with signals of their own. Whether or not these fish use electric messages in their courtship and mating is not known yet, but it seems likely that they do.

Spawning Time

The act of spawning itself varies greatly from group to group. Sometimes, as in herring, a whole group of fish may spawn while swimming close together. Male fish of many kinds use their modified fins to curl around the body of the female. The two fish tremble together as eggs and sperm are released. These males sometimes have special horny spots which develop on their bodies during the breeding season. Scientists think these roughened or spiny bumps help the male grip the female securely during spawning. In other species, the fish take turns. The female lays a few eggs, and the male fertilizes them while she waits. Then she lays another batch, and so forth.

Some fish, largely those in tropical places where the seasons vary little, reproduce all year around. Most species, however, have a definite spawning season. While many fish reproduce in their home area, others swim to special spawning sites. Salmon, fresh-water eels, and lampreys go on spectacularly long migrations, while many sea and lake species simply move into shallow waters. Fish which mate in large groups can produce quite an impressive sight. When the herring gather in San Francisco Bay to spawn, the water around piers and docks churns with their bodies. Sea gulls,

The sight of grunion spawning is an amazing one, and draws crowds of people to watch it during the high tides when it occurs.

pelicans, and other birds dive repeatedly at the water, feasting on the millions of animated fish, while humans watch with excited interest.

The grunion is famous for its predictable spawning. Grunion mating is synchronized with the phases of the moon and the tides. Between late February and early December, these small silvery fish leap up out of the water in vast numbers onto southern California beaches during high

tides. The female, with one or two males curled around her body, burrows quickly into the sand with her tail and lays her eggs, which are then fertilized. The tides wash more sand over the eggs, protecting them from enemies. The parent fish flop back into the sea, and the eggs develop in the moist sand. They are ready to hatch in about a week, but the young remain safely inside the eggs until the next high tide, two weeks after laying time. When the water again rises high on the beach, the infant grunions hatch out and are washed into the sea.

While the rhythms of the tides appear to synchronize grunion spawning, other environmental factors affect other fish. Those with annual reproductive cycles usually spawn in the spring or early summer, when food is abundant and time is available for the young to grow strong before colder, leaner times.

The increase in day length as spring approaches, combined with the warming up of the water, appears to stimulate the development of eggs and sperm. Many fish in regions with a wet and a dry season spawn in response to flooding of the land. In the laboratory, such fish will mate only if they are placed in water which has run over dry ground. Scientists suspect that an oil present in the sunbaked earth is carried away by the water and triggers spawning in such fish.

Unusual Mating

Some fish have totally different ways of getting the eggs and sperm together at the right time. The sea devils

The female sea devil, above, has a lighted lure that attracts prey and probably its mate (or mates) as well. The mate attaches itself to her underside and stays attached permanently.

have a unique method. These nightmarish creatures live in the dark depths of the ocean, where few animals can survive. Since there is no light, plants cannot grow. The fish which live in these regions must all feed on one another. Sea devils have special glowing outgrowths on their heads which they dangle in front of their mouths; these lure other fish.

Their gaping mouths with many sharp teeth can deal with large prey. Despite their fierce appearance, sea devils are not especially big. The largest known is only eighteen inches long—about 46 centimeters.

Only female sea devils have big mouths and lures, while the smaller males have pincer-like jaws and large eyes which look toward the front. The sense of smell of the young male sea devil is also highly developed. He swims freely until he finds a female, probably by the light of her lure and her odor. Then he grabs her with his sharp teeth and never lets go again. His skin fuses with hers, completely engulfing his mouth, except for a small opening on each side which allows water to enter for respiration. Their circulatory systems also unite, so that his body is nourished by hers. His eyes degenerate, and his smooth skin becomes spiny. He spends the rest of his life attached to his mate, insuring that whenever she spawns, her eggs will be fertilized. As many as three little males have been found attached to one female sea devil.

Two Sexes in One

We are used to thinking of animals as male or female. In humans and familiar animals such as dogs, cats, and birds, this is the way things are. But in certain creatures, one individual produces both sperm and eggs. Such animals are called hermaphrodites. Earthworms and some snails are hermaphrodites, for example. When they mate, each animal gives the other one sperm, so both are fertilized. Some kinds of hermaphrodites can fertilize themselves and never need to mate. A small minnow from Florida can reproduce perfectly well without ever encountering another of its kind. The eggs are fertilized inside the fish's body and are usually spawned within a day of being fertilized. In the laboratory, some fish lay eggs almost every day, taking from one to almost nine hours to deposit up to twelve eggs.

A small grouper common along the western Florida coast is hermaphroditic. These fish mate from spring through summer and have territories. Usually there are two fish in each territory. They are reddish brown with a pure white patch on the abdomen. When the fish are ready to spawn, the abdomen swells with eggs, making the white area stand out strikingly. One fish, usually the larger, takes on the female role first. It is pale in color. The fish which has the male role has broad, dark vertical bands on its body.

This one chases the other fish around in circles. Then the two of them swim up toward the surface, twist their bodies, and snap them sharply as they spawn and then straighten their bodies. The "female" fish leads in the swimming upward and, just before releasing the eggs, develops a banding pattern exactly the reverse of the male pattern. This probably acts as a signal to the other fish of the exact moment of spawning so that the eggs and sperm can be released at the same time. After the snap, the fish swim down again and may repeat the prespawning chase. This time they may reverse their roles and color patterns. Pairs can reverse their roles several times before the spawning session is over.

If both fish in the pair want to be the female first,

trouble results. They threaten each other by bending into S-shapes and showing each other their swollen white abdomens. They may also peck at one another until one fish finally gives up and develops the male banding pattern. Then they can mate. If a grouper is ready to spawn and has no mate to joint it, it simply releases both eggs and sperm by itself.

An Australian cleaner fish (these pick food off other sea animals) has a very efficient sexual system. Each male has his own territory which he defends against other males. He has a harem of three to six mature females living with him, as well as several younger fish. Each female, in turn, has her own smaller territory. The largest, oldest female lives in the center of the male's territory with the other females living around it. The male spends a great deal of time visiting his females and feeding in their areas. He attacks them and gives a special aggressive display in front of them. He directs most of his intimidating behavior toward the largest, oldest females.

If a male dies, something very strange happens. Within

These groupers are both male and female. The one temporarily taking the female role is seen leading in the top picture; middle, she makes a sharp turn toward her mate and then, bottom, they twist and snap their bodies, the female releasing eggs and the male releasing sperm. The two fish may then reverse their sex roles, the former male now releasing eggs and the former female fertilizing them.

two hours of his death, the largest female in his harem begins to show male behavior. Soon she is visiting the other
females and displaying male-type aggressive behavior to
them. Not only is "she" behaving like a male, she is becoming one. Within a few days this newly dominant fish
becomes a functioning male, and can spawn with the
females, fertilizing their eggs.

Only Females

Some fish manage to reproduce without any males at
all. A kind of goldfish, a molly, and several live-bearers
from Mexico function this way. The Mexican fish are of two
types, but all are female hybrids between two normal
species. In one type, the hybrid female has a normal number of chromosomes, the controllers of inheritance in cells.
She mates with a male of one parent species. His sperm
fertilizes her eggs, resulting in all female offspring. When
the eggs of those offspring become ready to be fertilized
themselves, the male chromosomes are discarded from the
eggs, leaving only those of the female. Only female offspring result from the fertilization of these eggs.

The other type of hybrid has three sets of chromosomes
instead of the normal two sets. When these females mate
with a male of one of the parental species, his sperm does
not combine with the eggs at all. They merely stimulate the
eggs to divide. The young fish are all perfect copies of their
mother.

All these types of fish may be found living together in

the same population. When given a choice, males of the two parent species clearly prefer to mate with females of their own kind. Then how do these peculiar hybrids manage to survive? Since they produce only females, every individual of the species bears young, whereas in a normal species, only half do. Therefore their reproduction is twice as efficient. Reluctant males are forced to mate with the hybrids, since one male of each parental species becomes dominant over the others. He prevents the other males from courting females of their own kind, so they must either mate with hybrids or not mate at all.

4 · How Fish Develop

The eggs which a female fish lays are produced in body organs called ovaries. These are located next to the kidneys. Most fish have two ovaries, one on each side; some species have only one. Even when millions of eggs develop at a time, each egg grows in its own place, called a follicle, separated from the other growing eggs. In the follicle the egg is surrounded by cells which provide it with nourishment. When spawning time comes, the eggs are released from their follicles into the cavity of the ovary. From there they move into the water through a passageway called the oviduct.

The cartilage fish have particularly well developed oviducts—large enough to accommodate the large, yolky eggs. Special glands in the walls produce the strong, horny shells which surround the eggs of egg-laying species. Sperm are stored in the oviduct after mating, too. The young of live-bearing cartilage fish develop in their mother's oviducts. In contrast, teleost fish have a short, simple duct which serves only as a way for the eggs to reach the outside.

The sperm develop in the testes. Sperm are produced in great quantity in all fish. They are minute cells which have a tail-like flagellum. The flagellum thrashes like a whip, propelling the sperm toward the eggs after they are released through the sperm ducts.

Teleost Development

Fertilization and development vary from one group of animals to another. We will describe what happens in only one fish group, the teleosts. Fertilization occurs when a sperm cell meets an egg cell and enters it. In teleosts, the egg itself is surrounded by an egg case called the chorion. There is a small hole in the chorion. It is so narrow that only one sperm can pass through at a time. When one sperm has entered, a plug forms in the hole and no more sperm can get in. The whole chorion hardens, producing a tough protective envelope for the developing embryo.

The egg itself consists of two parts, the living cytoplasm and the stored food called yolk, which will nourish the developing embryo. After fertilization, all the cytoplasm moves to the area of the egg near where the sperm entered. Teleost eggs have quite a bit of yolk, some more than others. But all have enough that the whole egg does not divide to form the embryo. Only the cap of cytoplasm divides, while the yolk remains in one mass. Even so, the cytoplasm does not divide completely. As the cells of the embryo divide and divide again, individual cells called blastomeres are formed above the yolk. But the cytoplasm next to the yolk

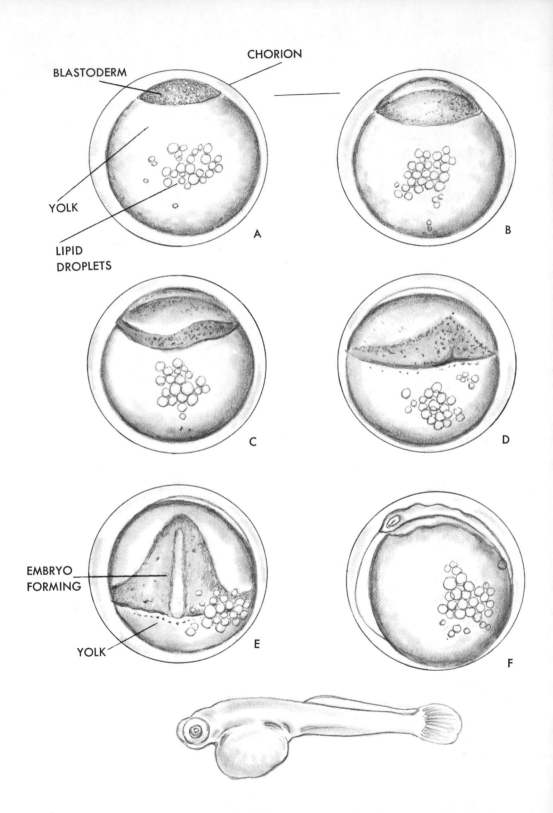

BLASTODERM

CHORION

YOLK

LIPID
DROPLETS

A

B

C

D

EMBRYO
FORMING

YOLK

E

F

does not divide into complete cells. This layer is called the periblast. It has many nuclei and is in direct contact with the yolk. The periblast tissue makes the yolk nutrients usable by the embryo. At this early stage the embryo, now called the blastoderm, is merely a mound of cells sitting on top of the periblast and has no structure.

After thousands of blastomeres have formed, they begin to spread out over the surface of the yolk. The periblast expands, too. During this time the embryonic cells move around the sides of the yolk and eventually surround it almost completely. Some of the blastomeres concentrate in one region, and this becomes the place where the embryo will develop.

As time goes on, the blastomeres form the embryonic fish. At first they are general cells which can become any one of a number of different kinds of cells. But as they divide further and form the embryo, they change into the more specialized cells of the fish body. Some become nerve cells, others become muscle cells, others skin, and so forth.

As the embryo develops, first the general body arrangement is laid out. The embryo looks like a fat, curved line

A fish egg develops. A, the blastoderm, made up of many blastomere cells, sits atop the yolk, which includes oily droplets. B, the blastoderm begins to spread; C, D, E, the blastoderm spreads increasingly over the yolk and some of its blastomeres concentrate into the "embryonic shield" from which the embryo forms; F, the developing embryo seen from the side; bottom, hatched young fish with yolk sac attached.

along the yolk. At the head end is the beginning of the brain. Along the body are clumps of tissue which will form muscles. Inside, the heart has begun to form as a simple tube. Next, the different body organs are formed. The circulatory system, digestive system, and nervous system develop. Soon the embryo has eyes, and its muscles can twitch.

When it is ready for hatching, the teleost fish is still a very underdeveloped creature. Some are ready to hatch a few days after laying, while others take several weeks or months. But in any case, most newly hatched teleosts are quite helpless and weak. They still have a big ball of yolk attached to their bellies and cannot swim. They look quite different from the adult fish, so they are called larvae.

After a few days the yolk is used up, and the young fish are able to swim and to feed. The larvae of many fishes live in a different environment than their parents do. They are likely to inhabit the shallow waters of lakes and oceans or live in the plankton. But wherever they live, the larvae of most fish gradually come to resemble their parents as they grow up. Young fish larvae have one continuous fin around their bodies instead of separate dorsal, tail, and anal fins. But as they grow, they develop the typical fin pattern of adult fish and are called fry.

Strange Babies

The planktonic larvae of many marine fish, however, are strikingly different from their parents. The young of

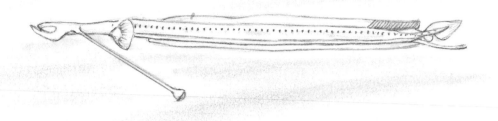

The strange larva of Idiacanthus fasciola, *with its eyes on the ends of long stalks. As the fish grows and descends to greater depths, the stalks draw in and loop themselves into capsules in the eye area—"as though there were no really good place to get rid of the curious structures," as marine biologist C. P. Idyll put it—though without obscuring its sight.*

one common deep-sea fish species, *Idiacanthus fasciola,* are especially strange. These small, delicate, transparent larvae have incredibly long eyestalks. A rod of cartilage supports each eye. There are muscles attached to the rod, and other thin muscles run along the stalk to the eye itself. These prominent, flexible eyes must help the little predator in its hunt for food among the sunlit plankton layers.

For years scientists thought the larvae was a completely different species from the adult. But the great pioneer oceanographer Dr. William Beebe carefully traced the metamorphosis of this unusual larva. As the little fish grows, the eyes are gradually withdrawn into a normal position. At the same time the larva gradually sinks from the well-lighted upper layers of the sea into the deeper, darker regions below.

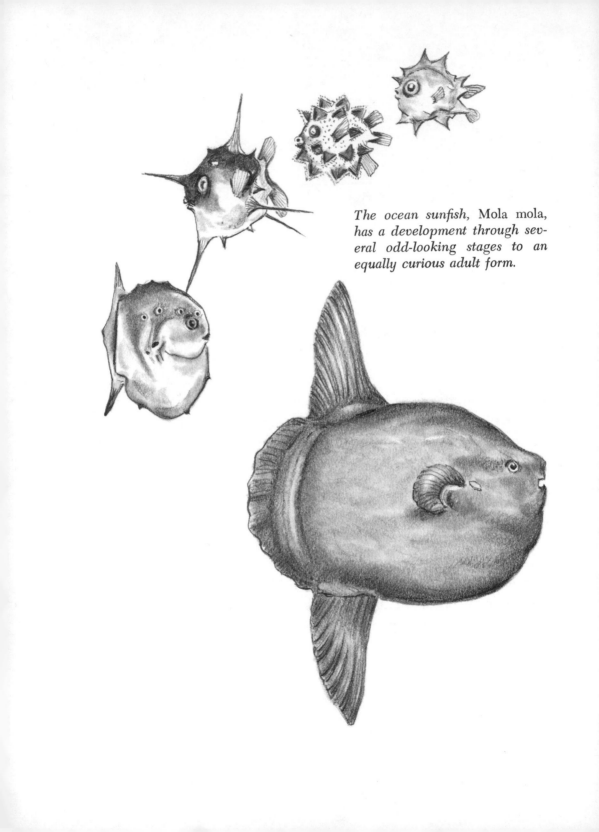

The ocean sunfish, Mola mola, has a development through several odd-looking stages to an equally curious adult form.

The larva of the ocean sunfish, on the other hand, changes form several times before it resembles the adult. The sunfish is one-eighth inch (about three millimeters) long, round and spiny, a prickly mouthful for a hungry enemy. As this armored little fellow grows, five of its spines become very long, thin, and sharp. By the time it is an inch long, the larva is a misshapen-looking creature with a deep but short body and hardly any fins. Eventually it reaches its final, equally strange adult shape. The flattened, oval body is almost tailless, while the dorsal and anal fins are elongated like a narrow sail and rudder. Despite its improbable appearance, the ocean sunfish manages to reach the length of eleven feet (nearly four meters) and a weight of one ton (about 907 kilograms). The huge female begins the cycle all over again when she lays as many as 300 million eggs.

The flounder is familiar as a food species. The adult spends its life lying on its side on the sea floor. But the young flounder is very different. When it hatches, it is a typical fish larva. After the yolk is absorbed it lives in the plankton, feeding on small animals there. After a month or so the little fish is about a half inch long. Remarkable changes now begin in its body. One eye begins to change position. Slowly but surely, it moves around the head until both eyes are on the same side of it. The larva begins to swim in a tilted position as well. The farther the eye moves, the more tilted the fish becomes, until it swims on its side. The mouth of some flatfish also becomes twisted, and the fins on the bottom side grow less than those on top. The fish leaves the plankton, taking up life on the bottom of the sea. The underside usually remains pale, while the upper side develops brown patterns which blend well with the bottom, making the fish almost impossible to see.

5 · Live-Bearing Fish

Since mammals are live-bearing, or viviparous, animals, fish with this kind of reproduction are of special interest to humans. Viviparity in fish is interesting also because it evolved independently in several fish groups. Besides the many viviparous cartilage fish, there are several families of live-bearing teleosts. The coelacanth, which is the one remaining fish of a very ancient, otherwise extinct group of fish, is also viviparous. Different adaptations of the embryo and the female fish are found in these different groups.

The first step toward viviparity is internal fertilization of the eggs. When the eggs are fertilized inside the body of the female, there is a greater chance that all of them will be fertilized than when the eggs and sperm are released into the water. There are other benefits, too. With internal fertilization, the female fish can mate at a convenient time before her eggs are ready to be fertilized. After mating, she can store the sperm until they are needed. In many species, mating occurs during the dry season. At this time it is easy for the male and female fish to find one another and mate. When the rainy season comes, the flooding which results stimulates the eggs to mature, and the female fish can spawn alone immediately without having to find a mate in the vast flooded area.

Despite its advantages, internal fertilization is relatively rare in fish. Some modification of the male body is necessary in order to transfer sperm into the female's reproductive tract. All cartilage fishes have internal fertilization. The pelvic fins of the male have been modified into pointed, grooved structures called claspers, which are used for sperm transfer. In male teleosts, either the anal fin is pointed and elongated, as in guppies and swordtails, or the end of the duct from which the sperm are released is enlarged and altered.

The simplest cases of viviparity are only a small step beyond internal fertilization and egg-laying. The eggs are fertilized inside the female fish and are merely kept there until they hatch. The eggs have enough yolk to nourish the developing embryos, and the infant fish are born looking very much like the small, helpless larvae of egg-laying fish. The young of many viviparous fish, however, are nourished by the body of the mother and are born relatively large and strong. In such cases, the reproductive tract of the female has been modified so that it can give nourishment, and the body of the embryo has been adapted to receive and use it. The waste products of the embryo's metabolism as it grows must also be transferred to the mother's bloodstream for disposal.

The Coelacanth

The coelacanth is called a living fossil for good reason. Until the first one was caught off the African coast in 1938, scientists thought coelacanths had been extinct for millions of years. The living animal is very similar to its fossil relatives. It has strong, lobed fins and a peculiar type of scales. An adult coelacanth measures about one and two-thirds meters, or some five feet in length, and weighs approximately 150 pounds, or some 68 kilograms. Despite the great interest in this unusual holdover from ancient times, few of these rare fish have been captured and little is known of their way of life.

However, part of the mystery of coelacanth reproduction was solved when a female was found with five well developed young in her oviducts. Each little fish had a big yolk sac. There were no special modifications of the oviducts for nourishing the young. Although much remains to be learned about the lives of these animals, we now know that these ancient fish bear live young.

Cartilage Fish

In viviparous cartilage fish, as in the coelacanth, the lower part of the oviduct is enlarged into a uterus, where the embryos develop. In many of these fish the eggs are very yolky and the mother does not provide nourishment to the young. The fluid in the uterus of these species is clear, thin, and plentiful. In kinds with less yolk, the

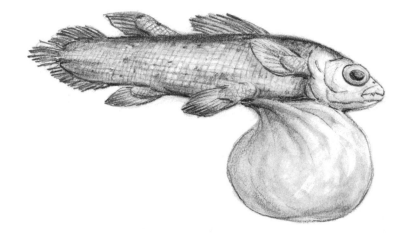

The coelacanth, a so-called living fossil, and its young, which hatch and develop fairly far inside the mother before being born. The fry gradually use up the sac of yolk for nourishment.

uterine fluid is thicker and cloudier and does nourish the young. This uterine "milk" is swallowed by embryos of the electric ray. These developing young fish digest their yolk in the intestine and the uterine milk in the stomach. Some ray embryos do not even need to swallow. The uterus of one kind of stingray has finger-like projections which grow right through the spiracles, or water inlets, of the embryos and extend down the esophagus, releasing nourishing secretions directly into the embryo's gut.

Highly developed viviparity is found in one kind of dogfish shark. Ridges grow from the uterine wall between the eggs. The ridges fuse so that each developing embryo is isolated in its own separate compartment. At first it lives on its yolk. As it grows, an elaborate system of blood vessels develops in the yolk sac walls, and the walls become folded. The uterine wall also becomes folded. Soon these two sets of folds become closely associated, the folds from the embryo sandwiched between those of the uterus. The outer cell layers of the folds also become quite thin, so that the blood vessels of mother and embryo are very close together. Now nourishment from her bloodstream can pass over to her offspring and waste products from its bloodstream can pass over to hers. Such a structure, in which the blood of mother and young are closely associated, is called a placenta. There is a stalk connecting the placenta with the embryo. The placenta of the dogfish shark bears a striking resemblance to the mammalian placenta, although it evolved completely independently. Other sharks, such as the hammerhead, also have a placenta.

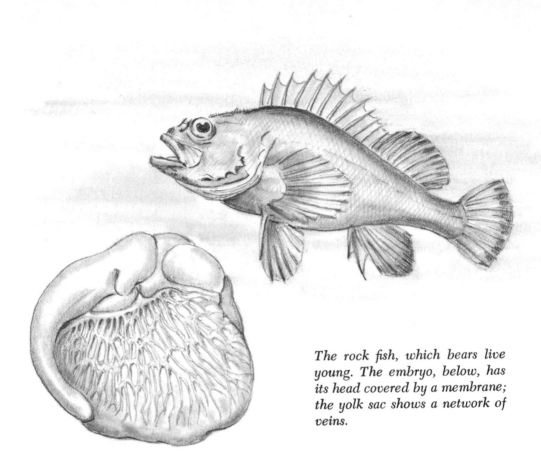

The rock fish, which bears live young. The embryo, below, has its head covered by a membrane; the yolk sac shows a network of veins.

Live-Bearing Teleosts

Teleosts also show all stages of viviparity. It has evolved separately in nine families found in a variety of environments. Viviparous teleosts are found in fresh and salt water; in dark caves and ocean depths; along bright shorelines and in warm, tropical lagoons; in swift, shallow streams and cold, deep lakes.

Since teleosts do not have the long glandular oviducts of cartilage fishes, the fertilized eggs develop inside the ovary itself. The embryos of some live-bearing teleosts develop individually right in the ovarian follicles. In other species the young develop in the cavity of the ovary.

The simplest kind of viviparity is found in rock fishes. The numerous embryos have enough yolk to nourish them throughout development, which occurs in the ovarian cavity. There is a good blood supply to the ovaries to carry away waste materials from the developing embryos. The young fish hatch from their eggs just before being born. They are yolkless and have well-developed jaws and eyes. They rise to the surface and live in the plankton, like the young of so many egg-laying teleosts. Although the eggs are protected from the dangers of life in the sea, the young larvae must suffer great losses—a large female of one rock fish may bear as many as two million young at one time!

Familiar Live-Bearers

The embryos of the popular live-bearing aquarium fish, such as guppies, mollies, and swordtails, develop inside the ovarian follicles. Their embryos have enough yolk to nourish them throughout development. The yolk sac, however, is enlarged and extends over the head. This provides a greater surface area for the exchange of waste materials from the embryo to the mother and oxygen from her to the embryo.

Some close relatives of these familiar fish have a more advanced form of viviparity. The wall of the follicle forms small finger-like projections called villi. The villi lie close

to the large blood vessels of the embryo, providing nourishment and exchange of gases. In a few of these species,
more than one brood of young develops in the ovaries at a
time. Sperm are stored by the females and fertilize groups
of eggs as they mature. In the dwarf topminnow, which is
barely 25 millimeters—about an inch—long, as many as
nine separate broods of young may be developing in the
ovaries at one time.

Four Eyes

The four-eyed fish of Mexico and Central America is
an unusual creature. Each eye is divided into two parts, one
adapted to water vision, the other to seeing in the air. These
fish spend most of their time floating on the water's surface
with the top halves of their eyes above the water, watching
for enemies.

Viviparity is well developed in these fish, for although
the eggs are small, a six-inch, or 15-centimeter, female can
give birth to young more than one-third that size. The veins
on the expanded yolk sac develop bulges called yolk-sac
bulbs. These bulbs increase the amount of blood which can
absorb oxygen and food from the liquid in the cavity of the
follicle. The walls of the follicle have many blood vessels
and also develop long villi which hang in the fluid or come
in contact with the embryo. The enlarged yolk sac and the
yolk-sac bulbs of the embryo, as well as the many blood
vessels and villi of the follicle, are all special structures
which make viviparity possible in the four-eyed fish.

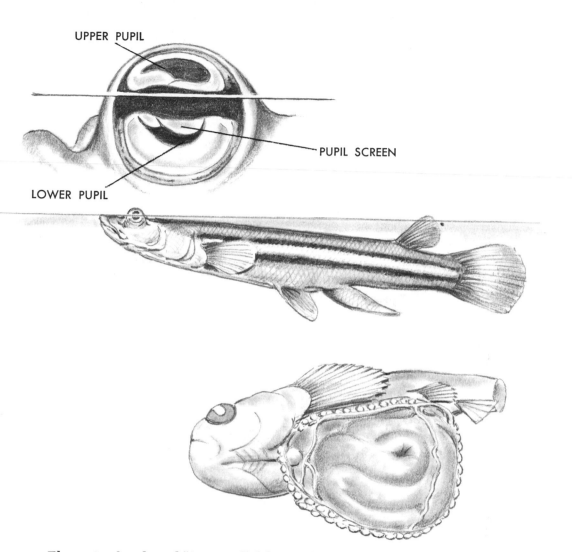

UPPER PUPIL

PUPIL SCREEN

LOWER PUPIL

The curiously adapted "four-eyed" fish Anableps and a cross-section of an eye half out of the water. The screen between the two pupils helps them to function separately by shutting out light either way. The embryo of the fish is seen below with belly sac dissected to expose the intestines, heart (sphere near head), and other organs. Around the outer layer are seen bead-shaped enlargements of blood vessels.

Incubation in the Ovarian Cavity

Other differences of the embryo and the ovary are found in fish with incubation in the ovarian cavity rather than in the follicles. In some of these there is a variety of ways to nourish the embryos. The ovary releases a nutritious fluid which the embryos swallow. They also swallow left-over sperm and the remains of embryos which die. Later in development, folds of the ovarian wall come in contact with the embryonic gills, nourishing the young fish by diffusion from the mother's bloodstream.

The embryos of other viviparous fishes develop long extentions from near the anus. The cells of these are very similar to the intestinal cells which absorb nutrients from food. These extensions disappear before birth. The ovarian walls of the mother fish are greatly folded, providing plenty of surface area for chemical exchange with the embryos. These folds are molded against every dent and bump of the embryos' bodies.

The Successful Sea Perch

Teleost live-bearing reaches its height in the sea perch, for the males of some species are, astonishingly, born ready to mate. The life cycle of these fish enables them to reproduce at the fastest possible rate. The shiner sea perch mates in June or July. Schools of older males, older females, young males, and young females remain apart most of the year. But the schools mix at mating time when they move into shallow water. The male performs a courtship dance in front of the female. She remains still while he swims in a figure-eight pattern, occasionally dashing away for a moment to chase off an intruder. The dance may last an hour. When mating time finally comes, the male faces the female and quivers, then his body becomes limp. The actual mating occurs so fast that no one is sure exactly how the male transfers sperm with his strangely developed anal fin.

After mating, the female stores the sperm until December, when the eggs are ready to be fertilized. A large female may carry as many as twenty young. The ovarian wall has many secretory cells and many blood vessels. The developing fish have villi in the intestine which aid in absorbing food from the ovarian fluid, which is constantly being swallowed. Their fins are provided with flattened extensions which increase their surface area, and the entire fin surface has many tiny blood vessels and ridges which increase their area further. Because of the resemblance of

The female shiner sea perch can carry as many as twenty developing young within its body.

the fin surfaces to typical gills, scientists think that the fins exchange respiratory gases while the intestine absorbs food.

The young sea perch are born in June or July and can feed within a few minutes of birth. The young females mate during their first summer and give birth to the offspring when only one year old.

6 · The Annual Fish

Living things are often found in the most unexpected places. The ability of life forms to adapt to extremes of climate and temperature is truly amazing. Hot springs and arctic snows harbor simple plants called algae. Many kinds of plants and animals have found ways to survive in the hot, dry desert or the harsh, frozen tundra. The range of habitats in which fish can survive and thrive is also varied. The four species of desert pupfish are found only in small hot springs and streams in the Death Valley region of California and nearby Nevada. They can survive temperatures as high as 108° F. (42° C) and as low as 38° F. (about 3° C). Some of them also live in water almost as salty as sea water. There are four families of fish which are almost entirely limited to life in the frigid waters of the antarctic. These animals can survive and function in water which is always near freezing.

But perhaps the most surprising place to find water animals is in temporary ponds and puddles, where the water dries up at least once a year. And yet samples of

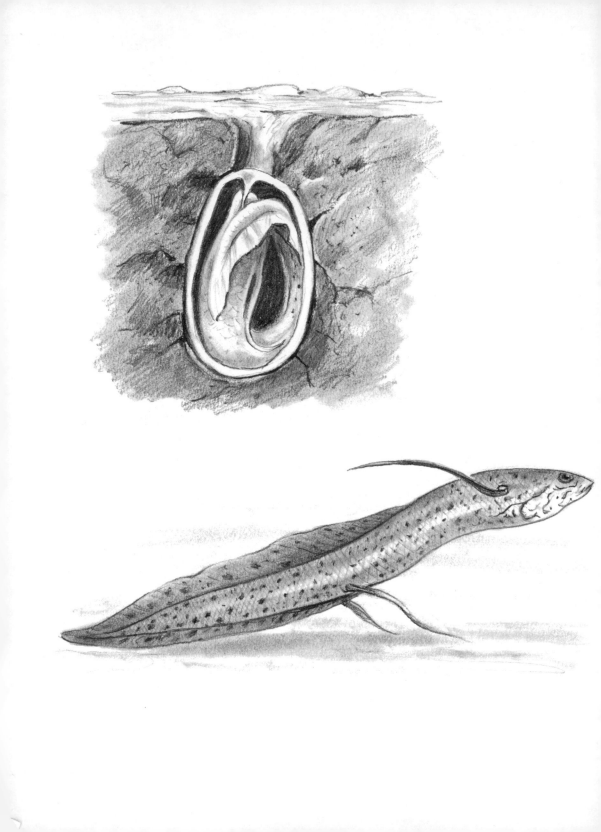

water from such places, even from rain gutters and old bird baths, show a startling variety of microscopic plant and invertebrate animal life. The creatures which inhabit such places survive over dry spells in different ways. In some kinds, such as the fascinating wheel animalcules, or rotifers, the adults merely dry up and remain in a state of suspended animation until water returns. Within a short time their bodies swell up again and they swim away, none the worse. Other kinds lay tough eggs with hard shells which resist drying and do not hatch until it is wet again. Plants of temporary ponds also produce small, resistant resting stages which can withstand extreme conditions.

But who would ever think that fish could also live in this kind of environment? How can they survive in places where the water dries up? Strangely, they can. Lungfish solved the problem of living in temporary waters three hundred million years ago. They evolved at a time when fresh-water habitats were drying up and they have changed little over the ages.

The African and South American lungfishes have well developed lungs. They actually get 95 per cent of their oxygen by gulping air, and die if they are forced to stay underwater. When its swampy home dries out, the lungfish wriggles down into the mud. Its skin secretes a tough waterproof cocoon. It lies there in the mud, with its tail over its

The African lungfish curls up in a cocoon during the dry season. Even after several years it can emerge alive from its muddy nest and resume its normal form and weight in a short time.

eyes, keeping them moist, until the rains fill the swamps again. During this time it breathes through a narrow tunnel leading to its mouth. This breathing tunnel is the only opening into the cozy, damp cocoon. The African lungfish can live in this resting state as long as four years. Its body becomes shrunken and shriveled, for its muscles are used to meet its reduced needs for nourishment during this time; in effect, they are eaten from within. But once it is again free in the water, it eats hungrily and quickly regains the lost weight.

Dying and Disappearing

The annual fish of Africa and South America live in ponds and ditches which dry up every year. No one would expect to find fish in such environments. For this reason, few people had even heard of the annual fishes before the 1950s; also, few scientists had looked in the right places. However, some German aquarium lovers had bred the beautiful pearlfish from Argentina. The female is pale with wavy brown markings, the male is a deep indigo blue, with rows of pearly white spots and a green iridescent shine. It was frustrating for their owners to find that these lovely fish, no matter how well cared for, became thin and listless before they were a year old. Then they died. Fortunately, the fish spawned willingly when given a mud-bottomed tank for breeding. So new generations of pearlfish were always there to replace their dead parents. And soon the reason for the death of the adults became known.

In their native Argentina the pearlfish simply disappear during the dry season. No adult can be found anywhere after the hot sun dries up their pond homes. Only the eggs survive, buried in the mud, until the rains again fill the ponds. Then the eggs hatch and the young grow rapidly to adulthood.

The pearlfish is only one of the many lovely kinds of annual fish. Because of their great beauty, many types of them have been kept by aquarists in this country as well as in Germany since the 1950s. In most species the female is dull in color but the male is gorgeous. All colors are displayed by annual fishes, in spots, stripes, and flecks. Some are delicately marked with pink, green, yellow, and red. Others have deep, rich reds, browns, greens, and blacks, set off by white streaks and specks. No other group of fish can beat their striking, short-lived beauty.

There are many known species of annual fishes, but more almost certainly are yet to be discovered. Some are restricted to perhaps a single temporary pond. These shallow, muddy, murky places may look uninviting, but one such pond may contain hundreds of fish. Some of the roadside ditches they live in look equally unfriendly, with water so shallow it can barely be seen among the thick water weeds. Most annual fish are small, from one inch (25 millimeters) to four inches long, but one giant reaches eleven inches. It must grow very fast to reach such a size in time to reproduce before the pond dries up. Although they thrive in unfriendly environments, annual fish are barely found in permanent bodies of water.

Despite annual fishes' curious life cycles, scientists have paid little attention to them. Only in recent years have a few investigators studied them. Their findings make clear why these fish are so successful despite their rugged environment.

How They Survive

An American scientist named John Wourms is responsible for most of our knowledge of annual-fish secrets. He studied mainly a fish with no common name. It has the long scientific name of *Austrofundulus myersi*. This fish is found in temporary ponds in Colombia, South America. Some of these ponds dry up once a year, and others dry up twice. The main dry season is from January to April. The second, and shorter, such period is from around the end of June to the end of August. During the summer, then, the fish must hatch, grow up, and spawn in three months.

The adult fish are two to three inches long. Six to eight weeks after hatching, they are fully adult and ready to breed. The female is a drab silvery olive color with some faint markings on her sides. The male is pretty, with pointed tips to his dorsal, anal, and tail fins. His body is greenish olive with creamy mottling, and his tail is metallic green and dark blue, with a brownish red border. He is a handsome fish indeed. His beauty does not last long, however, for he and his mate are old after a half year of life. But between reaching maturity and attaining old age, Austrofundulus in captivity spawns 25 to 30 eggs each day. There is every reason to believe that they spawn as much in the wild. So during her life each female fish lays at least 3000 eggs. Mating is relatively simple. The male and female quiver together side by side as the eggs are laid on the bottom. Fanning by their fins buries them in mud.

Although they dry out at some stage of development in nature, the eggs will develop completely normally if kept in water. But if one single batch of eggs, laid the same day by one female, is isolated, a strange thing happens. A couple of the eggs may hatch in forty days, but most of them do not. A few more may hatch in another month, but most will wait for several months before hatching, and they will hatch at different times during this period. Some may not hatch for almost a year. This is in contrast to the usual teleost eggs, which hatch a few days to a few weeks after being laid.

A Strange Embryo

Dr. Wourms studied the embryology of Austrofundulus to see why this was so. He found that the earliest stages of development were the same as for other teleost fish. But when the blastomeres spread over the surface of the yolk, a strange thing happens. Those that would ordinarily come together and form the early embryo in other teleosts continue to spread out instead, over the whole periblast. They are separated from one another and just distributed at random. No recognizable embryo forms for the present. Under unfavorable conditions, the embryos can remain in this stage, without developing further, for long periods of time. Such a resting period in development is called diapause. It is found at various life stages in many kinds of animals as a way of waiting out unfavorable conditions.

If the eggs remain in water with plenty of oxygen, the blastomeres remain spread out for several days. Then they slowly begin to come together again. In a few days, the shape of the developing embryo can be seen. Development then continues as in other teleosts.

Why should the blastomeres spread out instead of coming together to form the embryo during this period? Before they begin to form the organs of the embryo, blastomeres retain the ability to develop into various parts of the embryo. But once they have started to change into more specialized cell types, they are limited in their ability to form different tissues. Because of this, an embryo which had begun to form the body of a future fish might be too damaged by extremely dry conditions to survive. An embryo with dispersed cells, however, could lose many of these cells to drying conditions and still develop normally when it was again submerged in water. The embryonic fish would merely start out with fewer blastomeres, since some had died. Cell division would soon make up the difference.

Another adaptation of the annual-fish embryo to its harsh and unpredictable environment is the enveloping layer of cells which develops under the tough outer chorion. This layer comes to surround the whole developing egg and probably provides extra protection from drying out. It is shed at hatching.

At a later stage of development, the embryos of Austro-fundulus stop developing. They enter diapause again. This time, 90 per cent of the embryos stop developing no matter what the conditions of the environment. And they stop for a long time, as long as four months. When they start developing again, they do so at different times. Then again, just before hatching, almost all the embryos enter diapause again. While a developing embryo at this stage has a strong, beating heart and moves jerkily around inside the egg capsule, the diapausing embryos show little or no movement. Their hearts may twitch weakly but do not beat. They are in a stage of suspended animation which may last another four months. During this time they do not grow, and the yolk reserves are not used up. This diapause, too, varies in length.

Because of these three variable stages of diapause, the embryos will hatch at many different times. A very few may hatch after 40 days, while others will hatch any day between two months and almost a year after spawning. In this way, some young fish from any batch of eggs have a chance of hatching at a time when there is hope of growing up and spawning before the next dry spell. Even more variety is added to possible hatching dates by the fact that the female fish lays a batch of eggs each day over a period of several months. And since the embryos can probably remain in diapause as long as drought lasts, it is no wonder these fish can survive in their seemingly uninviting homes.

7 · The Long, Long Journey

Migration to a spawning area is common in fish. Some fish migrations are very short, as from the open waters of a lake to the shore. But some are truly spectacular, involving journeys of hundreds or even thousands of miles across the open ocean to faraway breeding grounds.

The Sea Lamprey

Although it can thrive as an adult in fresh water, the sea lamprey usually lives in the ocean. When it reaches maturity, it migrates to shallow-water streams to spawn. Though it is not a strong swimmer, since it lacks the paired fins of more advanced fish, the lamprey can still make it up low waterfalls by attaching its mouth to rocks and working its way upstream. Where the current is strong, the migrating lampreys move in the shallower water, wriggling violently against the current for a few moments, then resting.

Lampreys may arrive at spawning areas weeks before mating takes place. Males tend to arrive before females. They begin nest-building activities, and the females help when they get there. Nests are constructed in rocky areas. The lamprey attaches its sucker mouth to a stone. It vibrates its body violently, loosening the stone. The current carries the fish and its stone downstream a bit, where the lamprey lets go. It continues removing stones in this fashion until a depression is formed in the stream bottom, with a rim of large stones at the downstream side. The nest may be over four feet in diameter.

During mating, the male lamprey clutches the female's head with his mouth. Then he curls his body in a spiral around her. The eggs are laid and fertilized in small batches, so mating must be repeated many times. The eggs are sticky at first, and the activity of the adult fish stirs them up so that they filter down through the rocky nest, resting safely between the stones. After spawning is completed, the adult lampreys die.

About two weeks later, the eggs hatch into strange, primitive, toothless larvae called ammocoetes. The ammocoete is so different from the adult lamprey that it was thought to be an unrelated creature for many, many years. After hatching, the ammocoete drifts downstream until it comes to a suitable place to bury itself in the bottom. It wriggles down, covering itself completely so that only its mouth is at the surface. The mouth is surrounded by a fleshy extension called the oral hood. The hood protrudes from the burrow and captures small particles from the current. Water is pumped through the mouth and out of a series of gill slits along the body. Food particles are trapped in mucus inside the mouth and swallowed.

The animal may move around somewhat or even leave

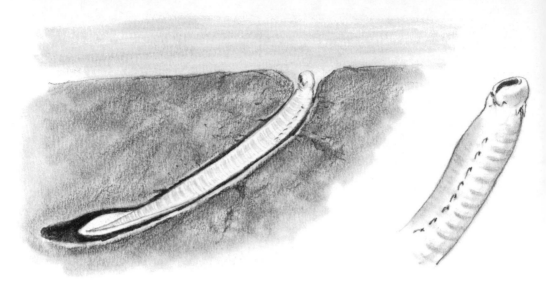

The ammocoete, the larva of the sea lamprey, has a fleshy oral hood lacking teeth; skin covers its eyes. The hood captures drifting food as the animal lies in a burrow.

its burrow at night. But basically, it lives a very uneventful life, buried in the bottom mud, straining food and growing slowly. It lives this way for several years. Transformation into an adult lamprey involves drastic changes. The small, useless eyes migrate to the surface of the head and grow. The oral hood disappears and the sucking mouth is formed. The flat body becomes rounded. Many other changes occur, and during this time the animal does not feed. It leaves the stream bed and migrates downstream to the sea, where it takes up the adult parasitic existence.

The Migration of Salmon

The migrating fish most familiar to Americans is the salmon. Seven species exist, one in the Atlantic and six in the Pacific. Upon reaching maturity, these fish may swim over 1000 miles through the ocean and up rivers, struggling against the strong current and leaping up waterfalls, to reach the stream of their birth. There, in the quiet shallows, they spawn. Pacific salmon make this journey only once, for they die soon after spawning. Atlantic salmon may go back to the sea and repeat their strenuous trip upstream several times during their lives.

How do the adult fish find their way back home to spawn? This mystery has always intrigued people, but the answer is only now being discovered. The great trek across the ocean is still a mystery. Perhaps the position of the sun in the sky is used as one guidepost. But since the salmon also travel at night, this can be only part of the answer. Once they reach the coast, the salmon are guided at least in part by scent. Their sense of smell is so keen that they can detect the unique scent of their home stream years after leaving it. (Nerves that do the detecting come from the odor-sensitive part of the brain, so scientists speak of "smell" rather than "taste.") Whether or not this ability aids them in finding the right river mouth is not known. But once they are struggling up the river against the current, they apparently choose which stream to enter by scent. Then they swim up until the next choice point, choose again, and continue until they reach their own birthplace.

At that point the water is sometimes so shallow that their backs are out of the water. They separate into pairs and the female begins to build the nest. She turns on her side and flexes her body, stirring up the sand. The current moves it downstream, so that a depression is gradually formed. Meanwhile the male may drive away intruding fish. In spawning, the pair nestles down on the bottom of the nest, after which the female digs some more, covering the eggs with sand. Then the parents die.

Spawning occurs in the fall. Hidden away under the sand, the eggs develop slowly during the winter. They hatch in spring, and the larvae struggle up through the pebbles until they come to rest on the stream bottom. After their yolk is absorbed, they feed on insects and other small stream creatures for some weeks.

The young of some salmon species drift downstream while still young fry. The Pacific pink salmon begins its migration right after hatching. But other kinds remain in the streams for up to four years, growing bigger and stronger all the time, before they begin their great ocean adventures. And, after one to seven years of wandering in the open sea, they too make the long and strenuous homeward journey to spawn and die.

The Mysterious Eels

A few fish species reverse the usual direction of migration. They live as adults in fresh water and migrate to the open sea to spawn. The most famous and amazing of these fish is the fresh-water eel. For centuries eel reproduction was a mystery. No one had ever seen a sexually mature eel, so it was supposed that they arose magically from the mud. Then through the nineteenth and early twentieth centuries, the eel story slowly unfolded. In 1856 a strange new marine

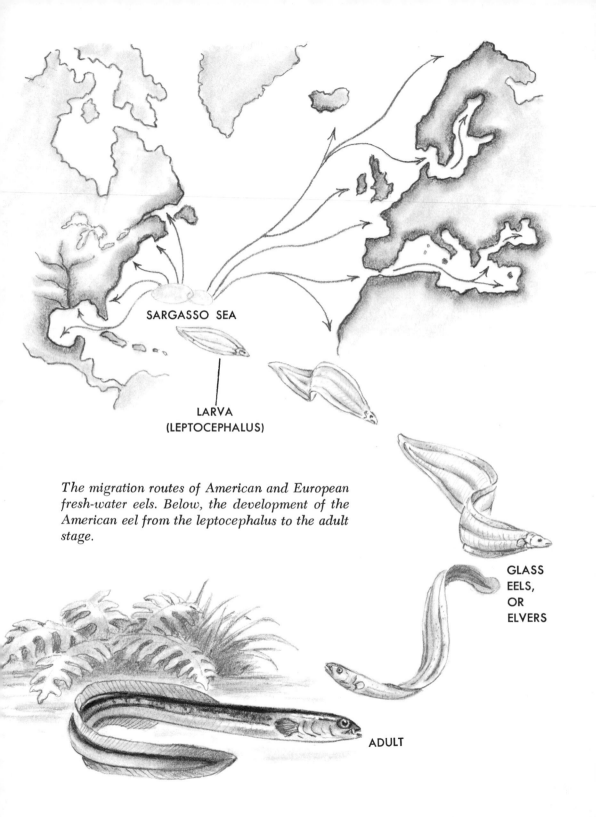

SARGASSO SEA

LARVA
(LEPTOCEPHALUS)

The migration routes of American and European fresh-water eels. Below, the development of the American eel from the leptocephalus to the adult stage.

GLASS
EELS,
OR
ELVERS

ADULT

creature, flat and transparent, was discovered off the Italian coast. It was dubbed Leptocephalus ("thin head"). But 40 years later, careful study of many of these leptocephali revealed that they were really larval eels, not a unique species. Then, in the early nineteenth century, a young Danish scientist painstakingly searched all over the North Atlantic Ocean, using fine-meshed nets and trawling at various depths, until he found that the nearer he collected to the Sargasso Sea, the smaller the larvae were. He came to the conclusion that all fresh-water eels from Europe and America swim out to the Sargasso Sea to spawn in deep water. This sea is an area of relatively still water southwest of Bermuda Island. The various currents of the Atlantic Ocean, such as the Gulf Stream, pass around it.

After hatching in the spring, the small, leaflike leptocephali drift westward with the Gulf Stream. A year later the American eels have reached our east coast. There they transform into rounded, transparent elvers, also called glass eels, about three inches, or 75 millimeters, long. The elvers swim up coastal rivers into the ponds and streams where they spend most of their lives. Meanwhile the European leptocephali drift northward up the American coast, across the Atlantic, and finally to the coasts of Europe, two years after their American relatives have entered fresh water. They are still flat leptocephali, but soon they too transform into elvers and invade European rivers, sometimes in huge swarms. It is remarkable that these two closely related species take such different times to reach metamorphosis. Nature has coordinated their development perfectly to fit the time it takes them to reach their adult homes.

While males reach a size of about half a meter (some one and a half feet) and an age of 13 or 14 years, the females are twice as large and may live to 23 years before returning to the sea to spawn. In fresh water, the eels are yellowish in color. They become silvery below as they migrate to the sea. Their digestive systems degenerate, and the eyes of the males double in size. They begin their long journey of 2000 to 3000 miles to the Sargasso Sea in the fall, where spawning occurs from late winter until summer. The adult fish then die, far from the streams and rivers where they spent most of their lives.

8 · The Fascinating Cichlids

Some of the most fascinating and complex patterns of fish family life are found in the cichlid family. Cichlids live in lakes and rivers of South America, Central America, Africa, and parts of Asia. Such familiar aquarium fish as the angelfish, firemouth, and pompadour fish are cichlids. Because of their interesting behavior and because many cichlids are important food fish, scientists have learned a great deal about these delightful and important animals.

Although most cichlids have fairly dull colors out of the breeding season, many develop spectacular breeding dress. The flaming red-orange jewel fish, with its iridescent blue spots; the Jack Dempsey fish, with its metallic green and blue spots against a dark background; and the flattened pompadour fish, marked in brilliant orange and blue, can all be seen in aquarium shops.

The colors of cichlids can be related to their natural homes. Species which live along sandy bottoms tend to be pale in color. Their breeding dress is often a light pastel color such as lime green or pale blue with a white breast.

Rock-dwelling species are generally dark in color and have vivid, iridescent breeding colors. Cichlids from murky waters tend to have orange or red markings, while those from clear waters are more likely to display blues and greens. A few species have bright colors at all times, while others lack spectacular colors. In species in which both parents care for the eggs and young, the color differences between the sexes are slight.

Mouth-Brooders

Many cichlid species, especially in Africa, have solved the problem of protecting eggs and young in an ingenious way. The parent fish, usually the mother, picks up the eggs in its mouth after spawning and keeps them there. Even after hatching, the young fish seek shelter in their mother's mouth until they are strong enough to fend for themselves. Besides protecting the eggs from being eaten by enemies, the mother's mouth is a fine incubation place. The eggs get plenty of oxygen from the water she sucks in for her own respiration. They are kept moving, so that the heavy yolk does not sink to one end of the eggs and disrupt normal development. This churning around also keeps the eggs free of mold.

Mouth-brooders living under different conditions have adapted to their various habitats. One common species in Lake Victoria lives in the open water most of the year. As the breeding season approaches, the adult male fish develop their breeding colors and move into shallow water. The same

Reproduction in mouth-brooders. (1) the pair make a nest; (2) eggs
are laid and (3) fertilized; (4) one fish (usually the female) picks the

eggs up in her mouth and (5) keeps them there until they hatch and are ready for the world; then (6) they are released.

areas of the shoreline are used year after year as breeding grounds. Each male stakes out a territory. Then, by fanning his pectoral fins and turning around and around, he sweeps out a small, shallow nest in the sandy bottom. Some other species make very large, complex nests, digging away the sand with their mouths. After it is dug, the nest is kept very clean by fanning with the fins. Bits of dirt may be picked up in the male's mouth and dumped outside the nest.

When the females are ready to breed, they visit the male nesting area and pick out a mate. They do not develop the fancy breeding dress of the males. Courtship is short and intense, and as each small batch of eggs is laid and fertilized, the female picks them up in her mouth. She may lay several hundred eggs. After mating is finished, the female leaves and swims to special rocky-bottom brooding grounds where she and the other females stay until the young fish are on their own. Meanwhile the male stays in his territory and mates with any other females he can attract.

The mother fish is busy brooding her eggs and young for 20 to 30 days. She does not eat at all before the young hatch, and sometimes not until she leaves them. When the young fish are released, they first live in the very shallow water at the lake shore. Here they eat small food organisms, and the warmer temperature of the shallow water may help speed their growth. Also, hungry predators cannot get at them easily there. As they grow, the fish remain together in schools and gradually move to deeper water among the weeds or near the sandy shore. Eventually the schools break up and the young fish move to even deeper water and live like adults.

While open-water species move shoreward to breed, rock-dwelling fish stay right at home. In Lake Malawi in Africa, several species of rockfish live crowded together in a limited area. They are mouth-brooders, and it is easy to see why. With many enemies around, the young fish can grow to a relatively safe size before being on their own. When danger threatens, they dash into the mother's mouth and are secure until the enemy passes. These fish lay a very few large eggs at a time. The female snaps them up immediately. The young which hatch from such large eggs are large themselves by the time the yolk is used up. In this way they are further along the road to independence before they must search for food.

Egg Dummies

We may wonder how the eggs of mouth-brooders can be properly fertilized if the female is in such a rush to snap up the eggs. Many of these fish have evolved amazing ways of dealing with this problem.

Male fish of some cichlid species have bright orange spots on their anal fins. Each spot is surrounded by a colorless, transparent ring. The rest of the fin is dark in color, and the orange spots stand out sharply. The function of these spots was discovered by a German scientist named Wolfgang Wickler. He noticed that after egg-laying, the female turns and picks up the eggs so fast that the male cannot have fertilized them yet. When he passes over the spawning site, the male fish spreads out his anal fin, displaying clearly the bright orange spots. The spots are the same size, color, and shape as the eggs. The female fish snaps at them, trying to collect them in her mouth. In the process, she invariably sucks in some sperm which the male fish releases as he displays the "egg dummies." Thus fertilization of the eggs is assured.

While males of several species of mouth-brooding cichlids have egg dummies on their anal fins, males of other kinds use other devices to insure fertilization. Males of a different genus grow a special structure called a "genital tassel" during the breeding season. This brightly colored structure resembles a whole clump of eggs. In trying to collect these egg dummies, the female fish collects sperm in her mouth. Males of still different species have elongated pelvic fins. The swollen tips resemble eggs in size and color and fool the female into snapping at them.

Substrate Spawners

All the cichlids in some African lakes are mouth-brooders. But other African species and most South American kinds lay their eggs on a rock, leaf, or in a pit in the sand. Such a base that an animal uses is a substrate, so these cichlids are called "substrate spawners." Their breeding behavior is quite different from that of mouth-brooders. The

Egg dummies are one of the many amazing adaptations that solve problems in the fish world. Some—the five examples at top and middle—are merely spots on the fins; in other cases, deceptive organs called tassels have evolved.

male and female are usually similar in color. Instead of a short, intense courtship after which the two fish separate, pairs of substrate spawners remain together, sharing in the care of their young. Mating behavior is less conspicuous and is calmer. The two fish become acquainted more slowly, sometimes over a period of several weeks.

A female angelfish, one of the substrate spawners, lays eggs on a rock that the mates have carefully cleaned; the male then fertilizes them.

Although the male is larger, both the male and female defend the territory before spawning. Together they prepare a place to lay the eggs by making a pit in the sand or by carefully cleaning a rock or root with their mouths until not a speck of dirt remains. The female lays the sticky eggs a few at a time. The male then passes over each group and fertilizes them. The whole spawning process may take several hours.

The eggs of substrate breeders are generally smaller than those of mouth-brooders. The female hovers over the eggs, fanning them with her pectoral fins. She removes dead embryos and dirt with her mouth. The young fish hatch after three or four days. The larvae still have some yolk. The parents move the helpless, quivering fry to a nest in the sand, either by sweeping them in with currents made with the fins or by carrying them in their mouths. The female fish stays near the young at most times, while the male may station himself a few feet away and chase off intruders. After a few days the fry can swim. They stay clumped together in a tight, wriggling ball. If any of them stray, a parent promptly returns them to the school. The length of time parents care for their young varies greatly. Some species guard them for a few days, while others protect their offspring for up to two months.

Fish "Milk"

The young of some Central and South American species get a special bonus from their parents. This unique aspect of parental behavior has been understood only relatively recently.

One such fish from the Amazon is the strikingly beautiful pompadour fish, also called the discus fish. These spectacular animals look like a product of an artist's imagination, rather than of nature. Their flattened, disk-shaped bodies are up to five inches long. Brilliant irregular blue markings decorate their olive-brown bodies, while their fins are edged in scarlet. These fish were introduced to aquarium keepers in 1933, and for years people tried unsuccessfully to raise the young in aquariums. Because a breeding pair was extremely valuable—one cost $350 in 1959—breeders did not want to risk leaving the parents with the young for fear they would eat them. So the parents would be removed to a separate tank. But despite all the care lavished on these precious infant fish, all of them usually died. Only occasionally a few survived.

In 1959 the reason for this problem was discovered. If the parents are left with their eggs and are not disturbed, they take turns guarding, fanning, and cleaning the eggs with their mouths. About four days after the baby fish hatch, they can swim weakly. At this time they all attach themselves to the body of one parent. As they hang there, they feed on a special mucus food produced by the parent's skin. The whole body of the parent fish is covered by this whitish material. If one parent tires of its hungry burden, it gives a flick of its body, thereby transferring the young fish to its mate. Sometimes the babies switch parents under their own power. For the first week the fry are completely dependent on the parents for food. After that they can eat other foods, but still nibble on the parents for another month or so. Gradually the parents' skin produces less and less mucus and the young fish become increasingly independent.

Recognizing One Another

Cichlid parents which guard their fry must be able to recognize them. And the young fish must be able to find their parents. An adult jewel fish recognizes the newly hatched, wriggling young by their scent. If wrigglers of another species are placed in the nest, eventually they will be recognized and eaten. After the young fish can swim, the parents respond to their color pattern instead of their odor. Adults will eat not only fry of other species but also young jewel fish which have been dyed another color.

The odor and color pattern of the young is learned by the parent jewel fish. If a pair of fish breeding for the first time is given eggs of another species in place of their own, they will protect them and raise the young. Then, if they breed again, they will eat their own young when they hatch. The adults have been fooled by the scientist; they have wrongly learned how to recognize their offspring. From then on, only fry of the different species are acceptable to them.

The young jewel fish, on the other hand, do not learn to recognize their parents. They have an innate tendency to follow red objects. They will even swim to a red disk waved near them in the water. An orange disk will also attract them. Young jewel fish show no interest in a dark blue disk, while a black one scares them away.

The young of some other cichlid species, however, will follow a black object. As one might imagine, the guarding parents of these kinds have a very dark pattern. The young of a species with yellow adults prefer yellow. A closely related kind has a black and yellow pattern. Sure enough, the young fish prefer models with both black and yellow markings.

Many mouth-brooding cichlids care for their young for a few weeks after hatching. The mother fish can signal danger to her offspring by fin movements which cause small currents in the water. The young swarm toward her, attracted to dark places and to crevices. They gather under her dark chin and around her gill openings as well as her mouth. But she backs up slowly in the water, gathering them in her mouth as she goes. When the female is ready to leave her young, her color pattern changes. She loses her dark chin patch, and the babies are no longer attracted to her.

The young of many cichlids form schools. They may have special conspicuous markings which enable them to recognize one another during the schooling period. Small cichlids of one species have dark stripes on their sides which disappear when they stop schooling. Others have a prominent black spot on the dorsal fin which goes away as the fish grow up. Scientists think that these special markings help the young fish find one another and keep together in a compact group.

9 · Protective Fish Fathers

In a great variety of fish which guard their eggs, the male fish alone takes on the job. Male bass and sunfish dig nests in the sand near the lakeshore for egg-laying and guard the spawn. Some male catfish incubate the eggs in their mouths, and the males of many goby species make nests under rocks or in shells which are guarded.

Two such families of fish with especially interesting habits have been studied in detail by scientists.

Sticklebacks

The little male stickleback is one of the best fish fathers there is. He spends hours carefully building a nest in which the female lays her eggs. After mating he guards the nest and the eggs. When the young hatch, males of most kinds take care of them for several days.

There are six species of sticklebacks. All have spiny fins which give them some protection against being eaten. When a predator attacks, the stickleback raises its spines, which can give the attacker painful wounds. Even so, sticklebacks are important food for birds and other fish. The various species range from marine kinds to those which live in fresh water. Some are found where rivers meet the sea and can live in either fresh or salt water. Species are named for the number of spines they have.

The three-spined stickleback is a favorite for scientific study. In the spring, males set up territories which they defend against one another. They develop bright red bellies as part of their breeding dress. They react very aggressively toward this color. The sight of a nearby male with a red belly makes a territorial male rush out and threaten him. If a red disk is introduced into his territory, a male three-spined stickleback will attack it violently. Even the sight of a red van driving along the street outside can make him bite furiously against the aquarium glass.

After establishing his territory, the male fish builds a nest on the bottom. First he digs a pit in the sand. Then he collects bits of plants to make the nest. He may test a piece of material by sucking it into his mouth and spitting it out again. If it rises or falls rapidly, it is not good enough for his nest. But if it floats gently in front of him, he picks it up again and takes it to the pit to add to his collection.

After he has gathered a few bits of nesting material, the fish glues it together. Part of each of his kidneys is modified in the breeding season to produce a special glue. He glides over the nest, pressing down slightly on the nesting material while letting out strands of glue. The nest is started from the rear of the sand pit. As he builds, the male pushes and pokes at the growing nest with his snout to shape it. He jabs at the front, making an entrance hole.

After five or six hours of hard work, the nest is completed. It is about two and a half inches long—some six centimeters. The male fish adds the finishing touch by boring carefully all the way through the center, making a

The glued-together nest of the three-spined stickleback is a nursery for eggs to which the male gives constant care by acting as a guard and fanning water over them.

tunnel with an exit hole as well as an entrance. Now he is ready to find a mate.

If a ripe female with a swollen belly swims by, the male fish gets very excited. He swims toward her in a zig-zag pattern, turning first sideways away from her, then making a quick zag toward her. After a brief pause he turns sideways again, and repeats. She is attracted by his dance and swims toward him with a peculiar head-up posture which signals her readiness to mate. Then he swims straight to the nest, and she follows. With his snout the male points to the nest entrance several times, turning slightly on his side to show off his brightly colored belly. The female accepts his invitation and wriggles into the nest. Her head sticks out one end and her tail out the other as she lays her clutch of 60 to 100 eggs. She struggles out of the nest; then the male enters and does his fertilizing.

If the female has not left on her own by now, the male chases her away. Then he tends to his nest. He jams the eggs down inside with his snout. Then he takes about 20 minutes to attach more plant pieces to the front of the nest, gradually narrowing the entrance hole back to its former size. When that job is finished he is ready to court the next ripe female that comes along.

Over the next several days, the male stickleback may mate with half a dozen more females. But with each passing day he becomes less interested in mating and more interested in caring for the eggs in his nest. His color darkens gradually, and the conspicuous red color of his belly disappears. It was important for him to stand out and be noticed while attracting mates. But now that he is guarding eggs, it is better if he is as inconspicuous as possible.

Besides protecting the eggs from hungry fish, the male stickleback fans them. He stations himself in front of the nest, forcing a stream of water over the top of the nest by beats of his pectoral fins. Strokes of his tail keep him from moving backward in the water. The water current passing across the top of the nest pulls water up through it, supplying the eggs with fresh water and plenty of oxygen.

In two or three weeks the eggs hatch. Before they do, the father fish may poke holes in the nest here and there, increasing the circulation of water to the developing embryos. Shortly before the eggs hatch, the male pulls the nest apart, yanking violently here and there until only a disorganized heap remains. In this way, plenty of oxygen is available to the helpless infants when they hatch.

For a few days the young fish just lie in the nest using up their yolk sacs. As they get stronger, they try to swim with little jerking movements. As these become stronger, some of the fry succeed in leaving the nest. But the father fish is close behind. He chases them and sucks them into his mouth, dashing back to the nest heap to blow them back in. Gradually the young fish begin to school together above it. They try to get away when the male attempts to retrieve them and they become better and better at escaping. This is a good thing, for a week or so after the eggs hatch, the father fish stops regarding the fry as something to protect. Now they are food to him, and instead of returning any captured fry to the nest, he swallows them.

Other Sticklebacks

The mating behavior of all sticklebacks shares certain features. The male sets up the territory, builds the nest, courts the female, and cares for the eggs by fanning them. Each species has its own characteristics. For example, the male ten-spined stickleback has a deep black belly instead of a red one. It has a longer courtship sequence than the three-spined species, and its nest is built among the plants instead of in a sand pit on the bottom.

The four-spined stickleback male has a silver-cream belly with red pelvic fins. Instead of doing a typical stickleback zigzag dance, the male does a spiral display, circling out from the female and leading toward the nest. He builds a cup-shaped nest among the plants. After mating with one female, he extends his nest upward, building another cup on top. If he mates with several females, he ends up with an apartment-house nest, with one layer of eggs stacked on top of another.

The structure of this nest requires a different method of fanning. After he has extended the nest upward, the male makes two holes with his snout on opposite sides of the previous nest. To fan the eggs, he sticks his snout into one of the holes and sucks water out, creating a current of water over that group of eggs. He must ventilate each clutch separately, and each "story" has its own pair of ventilation holes. The male spends a great deal of time moving from level to level, thoroughly oxygenating all the eggs. After one clutch hatches, he continues to fan the others until all the larvae have hatched. He does not pay any attention to them then. Unlike other stickleback fathers, he does not retrieve the young. He completely ignores them, not even trying to eat them.

Bubble-Nest Builders

Many people have heard of the betta, the famous Siamese fighting fish. It is one of the most beautiful of all aquarium fishes. The males come in a great variety of striking colors such as cornflower blue, purple, dark red, and glowing green. They have elegant, flowing fins, and move with a slow grace. A male Siamese fighting fish is ready for battle at any moment. When a mirror is placed against the aquarium glass, he will spread his fins and gill covers, displaying before his own image. Many, many years of selective breeding in captivity have developed these beautiful domesticated animals.

Although he is strikingly colored, the wild fighting fish is no match for his tame relative. He has ordinary short fins, barely longer than those of the female. His body is yellowish brown with a few metallic green markings. His dorsal fin is metallic green, too, with a red tip, and his tail is blue. His ventral fins are fiery red, tipped with white. The fighting instinct of the tame fish has also been increased by selective breeding. While two male tame fish can never be kept together in the same aquarium, wild males placed together in a tank may give up fighting after a few minutes.

The betta belongs to an interesting family called the

1

2

3

4

anabantids. Most anabantids are quite small fish, only a few inches long. They are found in Asia, with a few kinds in Africa as well. Many besides the betta are popular aquarium fish. The various gouramis are in this family. These fish are adapted to life in stale water. They have a special breathing organ called a labyrinth which acts as a lung to remove oxygen from the air. They go to the surface of the water frequently to take in a gulp of air. After a few minutes they return to get a fresh bubble and release the old one through the gills. They are also able to remove oxygen from the water with their gills, like other fish.

Living in stale water presents problems for raising young. As we have seen, various fish have different ways for providing their eggs with enough oxygen. Some lay eggs which float on the surface where there is plenty of oxygen. Others attach them to plant leaves which produce oxygen, and many different kinds fan their eggs with their fins, giving them a good supply of fresh, oxygen-rich water. The anabantids have a different solution. When he is ready to breed, a male anabantid builds a nest of bubbles on the surface of the water. He takes in air at the surface, coats it with mucus secreted in his mouth, and blows out bubbles from his mouth. They float to the surface, and soon a mound of bubbles a few inches across lies on the surface.

The Siamese fighting fish Betta splendens *mate (1); the female, turning upside down, drops her eggs (2), which are picked up by the male (3) and deposited at the surface in a nest of bubbles the male has blown with mucus. The eggs' position on the surface insures plenty of oxygen.*

The bubble nest forms the focus of the male fish's territory. When a female swims by, he spreads his fins to her. She may display hers to him in response. Each species of anabantid has its own courtship pattern. If the female is ready to spawn, she will follow the male to a spot below his nest. He then wraps himself around her so that his head and tail almost touch. As they sink in the water, the mating pair rolls over, and the female releases her eggs. The male fertilizes them. Then he lets go of the female and picks the eggs up in his mouth, blowing them with bubbles up toward the nest. This mating sequence is repeated many times until the female has laid all her eggs. The male then treats her as an intruder and chases her off.

Then he begins his fatherly duties, caring for the eggs. He must not only defend them, he must also make new bubbles every day, for the old ones gradually break down. If any eggs sink as a result of the bubbles' breaking, he retrieves them and blows them back up into the nest again.

After the young fish hatch, they remain in the nest until the yolk is absorbed, and the male still cares for them. When they can swim, a male of some species still cares for them for a week or so, keeping them in a compact school. Then he loses interest in them, unless he begins to see them as food. Males of some other kinds ignore the young fish as soon as they leave the bubble nest.

10 · Tropical Reef Fish

One of the richest habitats for fish life is the tropical reef. An incredible variety of wildly colorful fish from many families live around reefs, feeding on the great variety of life which shares these rocks with them. Almost all varieties of reproductive habits are found among reef fish. The surgeon fish, which get their name from the sharp, protective spines near their tails, usually spawn in small groups as they swim toward the surface. The floating eggs develop into transparent larvae quite unlike the adult. In many species, the young fish at a later stage are colored very differently from the adult. For example, the young blue tang is bright yellow, while the adult is blue. Sometimes even the shape of the adult is different. The adult bump-head surgeon has a large bump or blunt spear on its forehead, while the young fish have smooth foreheads.

The cardinal fish are very successful reef-dwellers, sometimes found in the thousands. They are mouth-brooders. In some kinds, the male carries the eggs, while in others the female does. Many kinds of sex-changing wrasses are also found living in these habitats. Some are cleaner fish, which set up special cleaning stations to which large fish come to have their parasites removed. The cleaners may even enter the mouths and gills of very large fishes without being eaten. So popular are their services that cleaners often have a line of fish waiting to be cleaned.

Damselfish

One family has been studied by many scientists. These are the damselfish, some of which are among the most beautiful of all reef fish. They are easy to study, for many kinds live in clear, shallow water. They are brightly colored and active by day, living close to the reef. A scientist with scuba diving gear can easily observe their behavior.

The whole range of territorial types is found in damselfish. The famous anemone fish spend their adult lives living among the tentacles of stinging sea anemones. They develop an immunity to the stings and can swim through the tentacles without being hurt. Any other fish would be stung, captured, and eaten. A mated pair of anemone fish sometimes claims one anemone for life, never straying more than a few inches from it.

Species of damselfish which live along the shallow, flat part of a reef tend to keep long-term territories around a nesting site. Males will use the same spot for a nest year after year. Even the young fish and females have territories. Other species use clam shells for spawning. The male fish cleans the shell carefully. When he is ready to spawn, the male develops bright breeding colors. Right after spawning, he loses his colorful breeding dress while he cares for the eggs. When they hatch, the larvae float up to live in the plankton. Shortly after they leave the nest, the male is ready to breed again, using the same shell.

Anemone fish can live among the protective tentacles of sea anemones without suffering from its stings.

The Sergeant Major Fish

The sergeant major is one of the most widely distributed of the damselfish. It is found in oceans around the world. Although not especially colorful, sergeant majors are immediately recognized by the black and white bars on their sides.

At night these fish hide among the coral reefs, but in the morning they form schools for feeding. During the breeding season they move to the outer edge of the reef after feeding. There they swim along the reef in one direction. Male fish investigate any caves or broken places. Several will leave the school at the same time. If they find satisfactory spots to set up their territories, they stay. Otherwise they rejoin the school and swim on.

As the males begin to search for nesting places, they develop a pale blue face and belly. This coloration spreads along the top of the head and the sides as they settle on a breeding area. Gradually the one or two dozen males which have colonized a cave in the reef begin to set up their individual territories. Within fifteen minutes of first entering the area, the males are hard at work claiming their own spots. They threaten, chase, and bite one another until the boundaries are settled. All the time their blue color becomes

The male sergeant major fish cleans away debris (1) for a nest and (2) leads a female to it; she spawns at the spot (3), the male immediately fertilizes the eggs and (4) guards them until they hatch. A nest contains thousands of eggs from a number of females.

more and more intense. The nonterritorial males which stay in the schools, however, lose the bit of blue they had and come to resemble the females.

The male carefully cleans a place for the eggs to be laid. He removes and carries off large animals such as hermit crabs. He bites the spines of sea urchins until they are annoyed enough to crawl away. He nips at the wall where the eggs will be placed, removing any surface material, and fans away sediment with his fins.

Within two hours of settling down, the males are ready to mate. Now they wait in their territories, watching for passing schools of sergeant majors. When a school appears, some of the male fish swim out to it, dipping and turning their bodies, making a wavy path. Then they turn around and swim slowly back to their places. Groups of females notice the displaying males and gather in front of their colonies. The females have the typical light and dark bars on their bodies, with a yellowish tint to their backs. The blue of the territorial males is now so dark it is almost black. Soon some females follow males to their territories while others hold back.

After leading a female to his territory, a male displays to her. He nips at the cleared nesting spot and fans his fins. The female presses her body against the spot. Now and then the male rushes out to defend his home. Soon the female begins to spawn as she presses against the cleaned place. The male then fertilizes the eggs. The pair circles around as the eggs are laid and fertilized in small groups. As soon as she finishes and leaves, the male invites new females in.

After several hours of spawning, the male has a nest of perhaps as many as 200,000 eggs to guard. He cleans around them and chases off other fish. His color gradually returns to the usual striped pattern. Four or five days after spawning, the eggs hatch. Each male leaves when all the eggs he has been guarding have hatched. Now the young fish must fend for themselves.

Many interesting fish-breeding habits remain to be studied. Despite their lowly position as "primitive" vertebrate animals, fish have developed a tremendous variety of ways to reproduce successfully in the various habitats they occupy. As scientists study more and more about their physiology and behavior, we will learn much more about these not-so-simple creatures.

Glossary

ammocoete   A lamprey larva

anal fin   The fin along the midline on the underside of a fish's body, near the tail

blastoderm   A mass of early embryonic cells

blastomeres   Early embryonic cells

breeding dress   Bright colors developed, usually by males, during the breeding season

chorion   The tough outer covering of a fish egg

cyclostomes   Primitive fish with jawless, sucking mouths, as lampreys and hagfish

diapause   A resting, inactive stage of an animal's life during which metabolism is reduced

dorsal fin   The fin along the midline on top of a fish's body

follicle   The place in the ovary where the egg grows

fry   Young fish

hermaphrodite   An organism with both ovaries and testes

lateral-line system   A special sensory system of fish that is sensitive to low-frequency vibrations

leptocephalus   A flat, transparent eel larva

ostracoderms The first armored, jawless vertebrates

oviduct The passageway from ovaries to outside the body

pectoral fins The paired fins located usually on the sides, just behind the gill covers

pelvic (or ventral) fins The paired fins located low on the body, between the pectoral and anal fins

periblast The undivided cytoplasm of an embryo next to the yolk

placenta The organ in which tissues of a mother and young are in close contact so wastes and nutrients can pass from the blood of one into the other's blood

placoderms Early fish with jaws and paired fins

plankton Plants and animals drifting near the water's surface; usually very small

spawn To release eggs or sperm (used for aquatic animals); as a noun, the fertilized eggs of one pair of fish from one mating

spiracles Modified pair of former gill slits of cartilage fish

teleosts The most plentiful family of modern fish

villi Small, finger-like projections of tissues, as in the ovaries of some live-bearing fish

viviparous Bearing live young

Suggested Reading

Books

Brian Curtis, *Life Story of the Fish* (Dover, N.Y., 1961)

Alan Fletcher, *Fishes and Their Young* (Addison-Wesley, Reading, Mass., 1974)

Mel Hunter, *How Fishes Began* (Collins-World, Cleveland, 1972)

Clarence Hylander, *Fishes and Their Ways* (Macmillan, N.Y., 1964)

Robert McClung, *Leaper, the Story of an Atlantic Salmon* (Morrow, N.Y., 1957)

F. D. Ommanney, *The Fishes* (Time-Life; Silver Burdett, Morristown, N.J., 1970)

John Waters, *The Mysterious Eel* (Hastings, N.Y., 1975)

William White, Jr., *The Angelfish: Its Life Cycle* (Sterling, N.Y., 1975)

———, *The Guppy: Its Life Cycle* (Sterling, N.Y., 1974)

———, *The Siamese Fighting Fish: Its Life Cycle—The Betta and Paradise Fish* (Sterling, N.Y., 1975)

See also books on keeping aquarium fish, and aquarium and aquatic-life magazines, such as *Tropical Fish Hobbyist, Salt Water Aquarium, Sea Frontiers, Sea Secrets, Underwater Naturalist, Oceans, Natural History, National Geographic.* These often have information on the breeding habits of fish.

Magazine Articles

J. Bouillon, "The Lungfish of Africa," *Natural History*, March 1961

Betty W. Carter, "Salmon Spectacle: Autumn Run of the Spawning Sockeye," *Smithsonian*, Oct. 1971

Eugenie Clark, "Mating of Groupers," *Natural History*, June 1965

——, "The Red Sea's Gardens of Eels," *National Geographic*, Nov. 1972

David Doubilet, "Rainbow World Beneath the Red Sea," *National Geographic*, Sept. 1975

Paul L. Fournier, "Migration in Maine," *Natural History*, Oct. 1964

Walter N. Hess, "Long Journey of the Dogfish," *Natural History*, Nov. 1964

Clarence P. Idyll, "The Incredible Salmon," *National Geographic*, Aug. 1968

——, "Grunion, the Fish that Spawns on Land," *National Geographic*, May 1969

Vicky McMillan, "Mating of the Fathead," *Natural History*, May 1972

Anthony Netboy, "Round Trip with the Salmon," *Natural History*, June 1969

Donn Eric Rosen, "Egg Retention: Pattern in Evolution," *Natural History*, Dec. 1962

Gene Wolfsheimer, "The Discus Fish Yields a Secret," *National Geographic*, May 1960

Index